IMAGES OF WAR

THE LUFTWAFFE IN WORLD WAR II

RARE PHOTOGRAPHS FROM WARTIME ARCHIVES

FRANCIS CROSBY

Pen & Sword
MILITARY

First published in Great Britain in 2005 by
PEN & SWORD MILITARY
an imprint of
Pen & Sword Books Ltd,
47 Church Street, Barnsley,
South Yorkshire.
S70 2AS

ISBN 1-84415-086-0

A CIP catalogue record for this book is available from the British Library

The photographs in this book have been obtained and reproduced with the kind permission
of the Imperial War Museum. The photograph captions indicate the reference number.

Designed and typeset (in 12pt Gill Sans Light)
by Sylvia Menzies, Pen & Sword Books Ltd

Printed and bound in Great Britain by CPI UK

Pen & Sword Books Ltd incorporates the imprints of Pen & Sword Aviation, Pen & Sword Naval,
Pen & Sword Military, Pen & Sword Select, Pen & Sword Military Classics, Leo Cooper,
Wharncliffe Local History,

For a complete list of Pen & Sword titles please contact:
PEN & SWORD BOOKS LIMITED
47 Church Street, Barnsley, South Yorkshire, S70 2AS, England.
E-mail: enquiries@pen-and-sword.co.uk
Website: www.pen-and-sword.co.uk

Contents

Introduction

Under the terms of the Versailles Treaty, Germany was forbidden to own and operate military aircraft. However, the design and manufacture of civil aircraft was permitted and pioneering names such as Hugo Junkers, Ernst Heinkel and Willy Messerschmitt continued to build the German aviation industry.

Even before Hitler came to power, plans were already in hand to build a new German Air Force. When Hitler became Führer he knew that he had to have a large, modern and powerful air force to carry out his aims. Ignoring the terms of the Treaty, the Air Ministry of the Reich was established on 5 May 1933 by which time a number of German military pilots had already graduated from a secret training base in Russia. The embryonic *Luftwaffe*, a well guarded secret, was made public and by 1936 over a third of German defence spending was allocated to the *Luftwaffe*. Hermann Goering commander-in-chief of the *Luftwaffe*, had ordered the production of a large number of modern fighter and bomber aircraft such as the Messerschmitt Bf109, the Messerschmitt Bf110, Junkers Ju87 Stuka, Heinkel He111 and the Dornier Do17. By 1937 Hitler could call on 1,000 fighters and 700 bombers – two years later Britain could only field the same number while the *Luftwaffe* had grown even more powerful. By 1938 Germany was producing 1,100 aircraft a year. During the invasion of Poland, the *Luftwaffe* deployed 1,750 bombers and 1,200 fighters.

From 1936 the aircraft and tactics of the *Luftwaffe* were tested in the Spanish Civil War and then became the leading element of the German Blitzkrieg as it raged through Western Europe. The confidence in, and of, the *Luftwaffe* was only undermined when the German air force faced the Royal Air Force on 'home turf' and failed to break the 'Tommies'. The *Luftwaffe*, to its end a tactical air arm structured to support land forces, lacked the strategic bombers with adequate protection essential to defeat a strong foe across the sea. The German air force had considerable success during the 1941 Operation *Barbarossa* against Russia. As in earlier attacks on Poland, Denmark and Holland, the *Luftwaffe* fared well against poorly defended targets and some German aces were able to rack up incredible victory totals such as Erich Hartmann who was credited with 352 victories. Unfortunately for Berlin, the propaganda claims of an imminent Soviet collapse never came true. Also, adherence to unwieldy heavy fighters types like the Bf110 did nothing to improve the *Luftwaffe*'s chance of success in an increasingly hostile aerial warfare environment.

Despite massive Allied bombing campaigns, Germany continued to increase aircraft production throughout the war. There were 10,800 aircraft built in 1940, 11,800 in 1941 and by 1944 39,800 were produced. Regardless of the types or numbers of aircraft produced, however, once the USA entered the war and brought types like the Mustang to battle, the *Luftwaffe* and Germany were doomed. While early in the war the *Luftwaffe*, in theory, had a slim chance of success through bombing British industry and removing Royal Air Force aircraft at source, there was no way that Germany could take on the industrial might of the USA who could build more Mustangs than the *Luftwaffe* could ever knock down. That said, Germany had plans for an aircraft that could have attacked the east coast of the United States. This aircraft was among many new types, some brilliant, many doomed but ultimately few of which made it from the drawing board to reality in the death throes of the Third Reich.

This book, featuring images from the Imperial War Museum's outstanding Photographic Archive, charts the successes and failures of Hitler's *Luftwaffe*. The photographs, many never before published, tell the stories of individuals, of aircraft and the German air force which at its peak was the largest, most modern and well-equipped air force in the world.

Francis Crosby, 2005

Acknowledgements

Special thanks are due to my good friends Martin Boswell and Peter Morrison.

Part One

Aircraft of the Luftwaffe

A British Air Ministry cockpit photograph taken of a Messerschmitt Bf109 captured intact. Pilots likened their position lying in the narrow cockpit of the Messerschmitt fighter to that of a racing car driver. From left to right, the elevator trim and flap trim wheels, tailwheel locking lever, throttle quadrant, ki-gas primer and then hood jettison lever. The instrument panel had its engine instruments on its right side and beneath it is another panel for the multi-channel radio and compass. The right of the cockpit housed electrical switches. Trainee pilots often received a surprising blow to the head as the unusually heavy side-hinged canopy was slammed closed. The Bf109 was the most famous German fighter of the Second World War having first flown in September 1935 powered by a Rolls-Royce Kestrel engine. In 1937 the fighter was first tested in combat during the Spanish Civil War with Germany's Condor Legion and in November that year the type set a new landplane speed record of 610kph/379mph. (IWM MH6665)

This Focke-Wulf Fw190 A-3, powered by a 1,570 hp BMW 801D was the personal aircraft of III/JG 2 Gruppen Adjutant *Oberleutnant* Armin Faber who, on 24 June 1942, landed at Pembrey in Wales. The German pilot apparently mistook the RAF airfield for his home base claiming to have confused the Bristol Channel with the English Channel. This was the first intact Fw190 to fall into the hands of the Royal Air Force and its evaluation proved most useful in developing means of countering the troublesome German fighter. The cowling of the aircraft bears the III Gruppe cockerel's head insignia and the vertical stripe on the fuselage just forward of the tail confirms the aircraft's operating unit. The chevron on the fuselage side denotes that the aircraft is flown by the Gruppen Adjutant. (IWM MH4190)

The Focke-Wulf Fw190 A-4/U8 fighter-bomber version of the Fw190 was powered by a BMW 801D-2 engine featuring MW50 injection which could produce 2,100hp for a maximum of ten minutes if required. The version (the U suffix stood for *Unrüst-Bausatz* meaning factory conversion set) was fitted with a Junkers-developed 300 litre drop tank beneath each wing and could carry a single SC500 500kg bomb under its centreline on a ventral bomb-rack. By the end of 1942 these aircraft were carrying out daylight low-level bombing raids against ports and cities in the south of England causing the Royal Air Force to maintain heavy fighter defences in response to the threat. (IWM HU2911)

This still taken from a *Luftwaffe* film shows the Messerschmitt Me323 Gigant (giant), one of the largest combat aircraft to take to the air during the Second World War. It was a remarkable aircraft developed from an unpowered heavy strategic glider intended for use in a planned invasion of Britain. To save on weight and aluminium, much of the Gigant's wing was made of plywood and fabric. The large and heavy glider had to be towed initially by a trio of Bf110 fighters and then by a dedicated five-engined Heinkel He111Z hybrid using two He111 fuselages joined by a common centre-wing section. The aircraft needed a great deal of power to lift off so to improve this, and increase the type's flexibility, a powered version was devised. All cargo entered up a ramp through the enormous clam-shell cargo doors in the nose. (IWM MH4183)

An early air-to-air study of a Messerschmitt Bf109 taken in November 1936. Created by a team under the leadership of Willy Messerschmitt, the type was the first all-metal stressed skin single-seat monoplane fighter with a retractable undercarriage to enter service. The aircraft pictured, the fourth prototype Bf109 V4, D-IOQY, was equipped with three machine guns, the weapon that fired through the propeller boss was later replaced by a 20mm cannon. In December 1936 this aircraft was sent to Spain for evaluation with the Condor Legion. Total production of the Bf109, including post-war builds, exceeded 35,000 making the fighter one of the most produced aircraft of all time. (IWM HU67699)

A Messerschmitt Bf109 G-6, fitted with a Daimler-Benz DB. 605 engine. As Allied bombing raids inflicted more and more damage on Germany's ability to wage war, a number of more effective weapons were developed to knock the enemy bombers from the sky and disrupt Allied bomber formations. The Bf109 G-6 was a dedicated bomber-destroyer fitted with the 21cm (8.27inch) rocket under each wing in place of the usual cannon. The rocket had a 90lb warhead and would destroy an aircraft on impact – fortunately for the Allied crews, the weapon was unguided and not very accurate. Nevertheless, the rocket would streak toward the Allied aircraft way beyond the reach of the 109's guns. After the rockets were fired, the empty tubes were jettisoned to restore the carrier aircraft's aerodynamics and increase top speed (IWM HU3245).

Designated Me323D and powered by six French-designed engines, deliveries of the powered version of the Gigant began in September 1942. The Me 323D could carry 9,750kg or 120 fully equipped troops over 1,000km. The type entered service in November 1942 flying across the Mediterranean to North Africa. In April 1943 a formation of 16 Gigants was attacked by RAF fighters and 14 were shot down. Improved armament and crew protection was introduced but nothing could hide the fact that the Gigant was a large, slow target. Losses caused the type to be withdrawn from service in the Mediterranean theatre but it continued to serve on the Eastern Front. The crew of five comprised two pilots, two flight engineers and a radio operator – two extra gunners could be carried as well. Total production, which ended in April 1944, amounted to 198. (IWM HU3033)

A Messerschmitt Bf109D pictured in 1939 with *schwarzgrün* (dark green) upper surfaces and fuselage sides and *hellblau* (light blue) under surfaces. This version of the famous fighter introduced the Daimler Benz 960hp DB 600 engine and saw action in Spain with the Condor Legion – some machines were also supplied to Switzerland and Hungary. Around 175 production models were made. The white shield insignia featuring a red 'R' denotes an aircraft of *Jagdegeschwader 2, 'Richthofen'*. (IWM HU38409)

Junkers Ju88 flying over Sicily. The Junkers bomber, said by many to be the most important German bomber of the Second World War, was in front line service from the start to the end of the Second World War. The Ju88 is widely described as the 'German Mosquito' because, like the de Havilland aircraft, the Ju88 was an extremely versatile design and was developed from a bomber for use in the close support, reconnaissance, heavy fighter, dive-bomber, torpedo-bomber and night fighter roles. In January 1936 the *ReichsLuftMinisterium* (RLM, the German Air Ministry) released specifications for a new fast bomber to carry a bomb load in excess of 500kg/1,100lb. The Junkers *Flugzeug und Motorenwerke* company responded with the Junkers Ju88 designed largely by two American nationals employed for their expertise in stressed skin construction. (IWM HU23910)

The cockpit of a Junkers Ju88. Construction of the Ju88 prototype began in May 1936 and the first flight of the Ju88-V1 took place on 21 December 1936. A total of five prototypes were built, and one, the Ju88-V5, made several record-breaking speed flights. In 1937, the specification was modified to include dive-bombing capabilities as well as an increased payload and range. The Ju 88-V6 was the first prototype built to meet the revised specification and it flew on 18 June 1938. In the autumn of 1938, the RLM chose the Ju88 to become the latest bomber to join the *Luftwaffe* and the Ju88A production version began to reach front line units in 1939. When war did eventually break out in September 1939, it was the Ju88A-1 that entered service although the first recorded mission was not flown until later in that month. The arrival of the Ju88 was a significant boost to Germany's bomber forces and, although it was heavier than both the Dornier Do17 and the Heinkel He111, even when it carried a substantial bomb load, it was still the fastest of the three. Unlike other *Luftwaffe* bomber types such the Heinkel He111, the Ju88 was not battle-tested in the Spanish Civil War. (IWM HU23907)

It took the installation of 1,000 hp Daimler Benz DB 600A engines and the improved all-round performance they bestowed to make the Heinkel He111 a viable military aircraft. The first mass-produced bomber versions, the He111E and He111F were desperately effective in the testing-ground of the Spanish Civil War where, as part of the Condor Legion, they flew in support of the Fascists. The effectiveness of Blitzkrieg tactics was due in no small part to the Heinkel bomber – the bombing of Guernica sent a clear message about the military might of the *Luftwaffe* around the world. The speed of the He111 enabled it to outpace many of the fighter aircraft pitted against it in Spain but this led the Germans to incorrectly assume that their bombers would reign supreme in the European war that was to come. (IWM HU23733)

A low-flying Focke-Wulf Fw44 Stieglitz (goldfinch) primary training aircraft pictured in 1938. As the Second World War went on, so the time spent on *Luftwaffe* pilot training was shortened. At the start of the war, having completed elementary flying school, trainee *Luftwaffe* pilots would have perhaps 150 hours flying time on a succession of types including the Fw44. If they graduated they would be awarded a pilot's licence as well as the coveted *Flugzeugführerabzeichen* – pilot's qualification badge. The Fw44 first flew in 1932 and was extensively used by the *Luftwaffe* who were impressed by its aerobatic capabilities. The type was also widely exported to nations including Chile, China and Turkey while licenced production was carried out in Argentina, Austria, Brazil, Bulgaria and Sweden. (IWM HU22433)

A Junkers Ju88A-5 of III/KG 30 'Adler'. The A-5 was a long-winged version of the Ju88A-1 and was used extensively during the Battle of Britain. The strong and manoeuvrable Ju88 was a key *Luftwaffe* aircraft in the 1940 Battle of Britain but, in spite of its speed, it suffered at the guns of the faster British fighters. Although the Ju88 had an extensive battery of machine guns for defence, all forward machine guns except, that operated by the pilot had to be operated by the Flight Engineer who had had to leap from one gun to another as British fighters assaulted the aircraft. As a result of combat experiences the bomber was modified to carry extra defensive guns as well as more armour to protect the crew. The A-series was the standard bomber version of the Ju88. (IWM HU22420)

An historic September 1940 photograph of the start of a daylight *Luftwaffe* bomber raid. Junkers Ju88As of 2/KG77 fly from their French base towards England during the Battle of Britain. The aircraft with the code letter "D" was the bomber flown by *Oberleutnant* Werner Lode. The Royal Air Force had acquired their first intact Ju88 on 28 July 1940 when an aircraft of 3/KG51 landed near Bexhill. The official report produced after evaluation concluded, *The Ju88 is obviously an extremely useful military machine, with good performance and load carrying qualities and excellent manoeuvrability for its size at high speeds. ...it is however not an easy aeroplane to operate, mainly owing to its high loading...inexperienced pilots must in particular take some time to get used to the approach and landing, especially with one engine dead.* (IWM HU22380)

Ju88As of KG 77 run up their engines at Gerbini, Sicily, 1942. Following the Italians inability to subdue the strategically important island of Malta, the Germans set about preparing to assault the island and stop the British Malta-launched attacks on enemy shipping in the region. The Germans insisted that their Italian ally allowed them use of their best airfields in Sicily – including Gerbini – from where they would launch their strikes. In March 1942 alone, 2,200 tons were dropped on targets on the island. The *Luftwaffe* also tried to starve the British out of Malta by attacking the convoys that supplied the beleaguered island. In August 1942, a well-escorted convoy of merchant ships bound for Malta was repeatedly attacked so that, of fourteen merchant ships, only five survived. (IWM HU22418)

A Dornier Do17Z of 2/KG77 lines up to receive fuel on Freux auxiliary airfield in Belgium, 1940. The first military examples of the Dornier design, the Do17E high-speed bomber and the Do17F long-range reconnaissance aircraft, entered service with the *Luftwaffe* and saw action during the Spanish Civil War. Both variants were powered by two BMW VI 12-cylinder V-type engines with the Do17 F having extra fuel tanks and two bomb bay cameras. Further development of the Do17 E&F types led to the Do17M medium bomber and the Do17P reconnaissance model powered by Bramo 323 radial engines. The definitive variant was the Do17Z with an extensively glazed cockpit, 'beetle' eye glazed nose and uprated Bramo 323 A-1 engines. Nicknamed the "Flying Pencil", over 500 Do17Z models were built and although this aircraft could outpace most contemporary fighters when it entered service with the *Luftwaffe* in 1940, it was soon considered obsolete after suffering heavy losses during the Battle of Britain. Nevertheless, early in the war as the Nazis swept through Poland, Norway, the Low Countries and France, the Do17 medium bomber was a key weapon in the German inventory. (IWM HU22377)

An early Heinkel 111B after a landing accident on an airfield in Germany. The prototype of the Heinkel He111 first flew in February 1935 and owed many of its design features to the earlier single-engine He70 which set eight world speed records in 1933. Designed in 1934 as a twin-engine high-speed transport and in 1935 revealed to the world as a civil airliner, the He111 was in fact secretly developed as the world's most advanced medium bomber. Six He111 C series airliners went into service with Lufthansa in 1936 but even the airliner versions served a military purpose as two He111s in Lufthansa markings flew secret photographic reconnaissance missions over the Soviet Union, France and Britain. (IWM HU22358)

Belgium's Blitzkrieg – Dornier Do17z of 2/KG77 pictured on Freux auxiliary airfield, 1940. In 1932 the German Ordnance Department development guidelines, issued to a number of leading German aircraft companies, called for the design and construction of a twin-engine medium bomber with a retractable undercarriage. Dornier designated the project Do17 and covered up the military aspects of the development by describing the aircraft as a fast mail-plane for Deutsche Lufthansa and also a freight carrier for the German State Railways. On 17 May 1933 the go ahead was given for the construction of two prototypes. One a high-speed commercial aircraft and the other for 'freight' with special equipment – in other words, a bomber. The Do.17 bomber prototype first flew in November 1934 and its superior performance caused much concern outside Germany. At the International Air Show at Dubendorf, Switzerland, in 1937, the Do17 MV1 proved to be the leader in its class. It even outpaced a number of European countries' frontline day-fighters, including those of France and Czechoslovakia. (IWM HU22351)

Stukas in Bulgaria. Over 400 *Luftwaffe* aircraft gathered in Bulgaria in early 1941 to support the Italian invasion of Greece. When the pro-Nazi Yugoslav government was toppled, the Führer ordered another 600 combat aircraft flown to Bulgaria and Romania for an ambitious double strike. On 6 April 1941, having complete air superiority, the *Luftwaffe* was able to cover the simultaneous invasions of Greece and Yugoslavia. Both countries fell swiftly and the entire operation was over by the end of April 1941. The speed of these successful campaigns, and the earlier successes of the Blitzkrieg in the West, led the Führer and Göring to believe that the German Air Force could support any operation, regardless of complexity. (IWM HU24809)

The Sovereign of Bulgaria, Tsar Boris with senior German officers during an inspection at a Bulgaria-based Stuka Gruppe. Bulgaria had chosen to align itself with Nazi Germany in the spring of 1941 possibly to avert an all-out invasion. Although pro-German, Bulgaria did not take part in the Second World War with its armed forces and Boris refused to send his troops to fight alongside German troops on the Eastern front. Tsar Boris died suddenly after a meeting with Hitler and speculation abounds that he was poisoned for not being more cooperative. It would appear that Boris also resisted the Nazi call for Bulgarian Jews to be sent to Polish concentration camps. Bulgaria itself received 12 R-series Junkers Ju87s in 1942, followed in 1943 by 32 Ju87D-5s. They were used against partisans within Bulgaria and some may have seen action against German forces after the surrender of Bulgaria in September 1944. (IWM HU24810)

The German wartime caption for this photograph read, *The brilliant German airplane designer, Professor Messerschmitt has created formidable war planes in the extremely successful fighter planes Me 109 and Me 110, which can operate with success over the North Sea. A formidable weapon against England.* The aircraft pictured is in fact the little known Messerschmitt Bf162. This aircraft, developed from the Bf110 fighter but with few common parts, was created to meet a requirement for a *Schnellbomber* or fast bomber. The type first flew in early 1937. Unofficially named Jaguar, only three prototypes were built before the project was abandoned when the Junkers submission, the Ju88, won the contract. (IWM MH2626)

The Fw200 Condor maritime reconnaissance bomber had its origins in a Deutsche Lufthansa airliner. The aircraft grabbed headlines in 1937 and set numerous pre-war non-stop record flights from Germany to New York and Tokyo. Finland, Denmark and Brazil ordered the airliner but the military capabilities of the large aircraft were first spotted by the Japanese who were first to ask for a military long-range maritime-reconnaissance version. The first *Luftwaffe* unit (and its main operator for the war) to receive the Condor was *Kampfgeschwader* (KG) 40 in April 1940. By the end of September, the Condors had sunk 90,000 tons of Allied shipping and Churchill soon referred to these aircraft as "...the scourge of the Atlantic". Not only could the Condor attack a ship on its own, it could also direct U-boats towards convoys. The wartime German caption for this photo read, *...carries a heavy load of bombs over long distances and is strongly armed. It has proved itself, in a short time, a good weapon against England.* The Condor's reign ended in late 1944 as the Allies overran *Luftwaffe* bases in France. (IWM MH2627)

Ju88s in Sicily. These torpedo bombers were pitted against the British convoys that sailed for Malta. About 20 Ju88As had been sold to Finland in 1939 and mass production of the Ju88 started in 1940 with the A-4. By the end of the war, seventeen different subtypes of the Ju88A had been designed. One of the most bizarre came from a 1944 RLM request to Junkers to develop a composite aircraft consisting of a fighter aircraft mounted on top of an unmanned heavy bomber aircraft. This Mistel combination aircraft was then flown to the target, where the fighter's pilot released the bomber, which was filled with explosives and plummeted to earth while the fighter returned to base. These Mistel weapons used old Ju88s coupled to Messerschmitt Bf109s or Focke Wulf Fw190s. About 85 Mistel combinations were built by the end of the war but only a few missions were flown. (IWM MH24406)

Luftwaffe ground crew tend a Messerschmitt Bf109 minus its engine cowling. The 109, derived in part from the four seat Bf108 Taifun, was the aircraft flown by most *Luftwaffe* aces and the type was responsible for more kills than any other German fighter aircraft. Bf109Bs were first delivered to the Luftwaffe's 'top guns' *Jagdgeschwader* 2 *'Richthofen'* in 1937 and before the year was out, the aircraft were in action in Spain. Also, in November that year, the type set a new world landplane speed record of 379.38mph. Meanwhile on the ground, the Bf109 had an outward-retracting narrow track undercarriage that proved unforgiving during ground handling. (IWM HU92188)

Men and machines of *Kampfgeschwader* 51 *'Edelweiss'* pictured early in the Second World War. Notice the special winter shelters erected around the engines of the nearest Ju88 to give ground crew some shelter from the elements while working on the aircraft's engines. The unit's distinctive edelweiss flower badge can be seen on the starboard side of the nose of the Ju88A, half covered by the protective tarpaulin stretched over the cockpit. Established in May 1939, during the course of the war KG 51 also operated Dornier Do17s, Heinkel He111s and Me410s and took part in the campaigns against Poland, France, Britain, the Soviet Union and Greece. (IWM HU92189)

After an early war mission, ground crew prepare to get a Stuka ready for its next sortie. With air superiority achieved against obsolete fighters in Poland and the Low Countries, the Stuka was able to hold its own. However, when it came up against the Hurricanes and Spitfires of the RAF large numbers were destroyed on missions across the English Channel. The Ju87 had a slow top speed nor could it climb away quickly. Accordingly the Stuka was withdrawn from operations against the UK but the type continued to serve in Greece, Crete, North Africa, Malta and on the Eastern Front. On commencing a dive attack, the pilot adjusted the dive angle manually by referring to red indicator lines painted on the canopy showing 60, 75 and 80 degrees from horizontal. The pilot would visually aim the aircraft at his target until a signal light on the altimeter illuminated telling the pilot to press the bomb-release button on the top of the control column. The automatic pull-out would commence as the bombs left their cradles. The bombs would follow the same course to the target as the aircraft had during its dive, while the pilot would experience around 6g, frequently blacking out, as the aircraft automatically levelled out to begin its climb skywards. (IWM HU92190)

The commander (with the lifejacket) of a moored Bv138 flying boat reports to his squadron commander after returning from a flight. The aircraft commander is wearing a *Flieger-Schutzanzug für Sommer* lightweight one-piece dark tan coloured cotton Type K So/34 summer flying suit. The ground crew is already at work servicing the aircraft and making her ready for the next flight. A crewman can be seen standing on a fairing that replaced a deleted bow gun-turret which typically housed a 20mm cannon. Designed as a long-range maritime reconnaissance flying boat, the type, however, first saw action transporting troops during the Norway campaign of 1940. With a range of around 4,000 kilometres fully loaded, the Bv138 could range over large areas of ocean for up to sixteen hours in search of enemy convoys and shipping. Note the Blohm und Voss manufacturer's logo on the starboard side of the aircraft's nose. (IWM HU92191)

Stuka crews at play in Norway. The Stuka (short for *Sturzkampfflugzeug* or dive bomber) is one of the best-known wartime Luftwaffe-combat types and certainly the easiest to recognise with inverted gull wings and fixed undercarriage. Like many *Luftwaffe* aircraft, the Ju87 was designed to provide tactical support to the army in land actions. German strategists saw the potential of the dive bomber as an effective weapon when used in close support of ground forces, reducing the enemy's resistance before ground forces advanced. The Ju87 prototype was powered, ironically as later events proved, by a Rolls-Royce Kestrel engine and had its maiden flight in May 1935. The *Luftwaffe* was very impressed by the potent new dive bomber and, with testing complete, the Stuka entered service in 1937. The early Stukas were sent to Spain for operational evaluation with the German Condor Legion. In the first production version, the Ju87A-1, a single fin replaced the two of the prototype, dive brakes were fitted to the outer wings and the British engine was replaced by a Junkers Jumo 210Ca 640hp engine. By early 1939, all the A series aircraft were relegated to training duties and all dive bomber units began equipping with the more powerful Ju87B series powered by the 1,200hp Jumo 211Da direct injection engine. The B-2 was improved further and could carry up to 1,000kg of bombs. The D series fitted with the 1,410hp Jumo 211J-1 engine introduced more armour to protect the crew. (IWM HU92192)

Heinkel He162 Salamander and personnel pictured at Leck in Northern Germany, May 1945. While the He162 was being developed at breakneck speed, Hitler Youth were being hurriedly trained in gliders as pilots for the new interceptor – ominously for them, their training was to be completed by flying the new aircraft in action. Experienced fighter pilots may have been able to handle the demanding He162, but poorly trained Hitler Youth would not have fared so well. The first aircraft were delivered for operational evaluation and trials in January 1945, only three to four weeks since the type's first flight. In February 1945, I/JG1 became the first unit to relinquish, possibly reluctantly, their Fw190s to begin conversion to the Salamander. One Gruppe of three squadrons was formed on 4 May 1945 at Leck in Schleswig-Holstein but the airfield (pictured) was captured by the British only four days later. Fuel shortages and general chaos had prevented the fighter from ever firing its twin 20mm cannon in anger.

A Heinkel He177A-5. Between January and March 1944, the Luftwaffe's KG40 and KG100 equipped with He177s carried out what were known as the *Steinbock* raids. These revenge raids against London were in response to the Allies escalating attacks against German cities. The planners knew the single most effective way that the bomber could attack and hope to evade interception by the Royal Air Force's increasingly efficient night fighter force. The bomber climbed to around 9,000m over the coast of Europe and then, at full power began a shallow dive towards Britain. By the time the aircraft were over England they were at speeds of around 700kph/435mph which made the aircraft hard to catch but did little for bombing accuracy. The Steinbock raids were ineffective and although, of 35 aircraft that took part in the numerous raids, only four were destroyed by British defences, many had to turn back due to engine fires and other malfunctions. Following the D-Day landings, He177 anti-shipping missions from France ceased but the type was still in use as a missile launch platform against the Allies in early 1945. On the Eastern Front, KG4 and KG50 were first to use the He177 in the pure bomber role with some aircraft also being fitted with huge 50 or even 75mm anti-tank guns. (IWM HU4988)

He111-H-6s under production at the Heinkel plant at Rostock, Marienehe. One obvious way for the British to reduce the threat of German bombers was to destroy them at source by attacking the German aircraft factories. On the night of 23-24 April 1942 a mixed force of British bombers including 93 Wellingtons, 31 Stirlings, 19 Whitleys, 11 Hampdens, 6 Manchesters, and 1 Lancaster carried out the first of four raids on this Baltic port town. Some of the bombers were detailed to attempt a precision attack on the Heinkel aircraft factory on the southern outskirts of Rostock. Bombing conditions were good but subsequent reconnaissance missions showed that the results of the raid were disappointing and most bombs fell some distance away. (IWM HU5012)

Although around 200 Heinkel He 162 Volksjägers were completed by the end of the War, a further 800 were under production at underground factories like the one pictured near Vienna. The aircraft's light metal alloy streamlined fuselage had a moulded plywood nose and its one-piece wooden wing was metal-tipped. The He162 cockpit was modern-looking with an upward hinged canopy and an ejection seat. Maintenance was not judged to be an issue as damaged or unserviceable aircraft would have simply been replaced by one of the many new ones in mass production. The engine was top mounted to save on the design and construction time required to create an aircraft around an engine. Fixed to the aircraft by three large bolts, the engine's location did not cause aerodynamic problems but did affect stability making the aircraft difficult to fly and fight in. An onboard two-stroke piston engine was used as a starter motor. Production, fed by a network of sub-contractors including woodworkers and furniture makers, was expected to reach a peak of 4,000 per month. 140 main factories and hundreds of smaller factories were to take part in the mass production of aircraft. (IWM HU5010)

A casual observer would be forgiven for thinking the six-seat He177 had two engines but on closer inspection each Daimler Benz DB-610 engine is in fact a pair of coupled DB 605 engines driving a single propeller shaft. The designers decided that was a good way to reduce drag but any benefits were far outweighed by the many problems caused by these troublesome engines which regularly caught fire in the air. Six out of the eight prototypes crashed and out of the first 35 pre-production A-0 models built mainly by Arado, many were written off due to take-off accidents or fires in flight. A further 130 A-1 version was built by Arado while Heinkel were responsible for the production of the A-3 and A-5 versions of which 170 and 826 were constructed respectively. The aircraft itself was essentially a good design and the slim tubular fuselage and long wings gave a range of 5,500km/3,417miles, far beyond anything else in the *Luftwaffe* inventory. The engine was the design's Achilles Heel and plagued its service record. The type, in A-1 form was first used in action by KG (*Kampfgeschwader*) 40 for maritime strike and reconnaissance missions. from bases in France. The aircraft pictured is a Heinkel He177A-03 pre-production example taxiing out for a test flight. (IWM HU5014)

The Sicilian local seems more interested in the camera than the bombed-up Junkers Ju88A-4 he is passing. The aircraft is there no doubt as part of the *Luftwaffe* bomber force that attempted to pound Malta into oblivion. The A-4 was one of the most numerous versions and the one from which many others derived. The four-seat bomber (note the four crew in the photo) had a long-span wing to carry heavier bomb loads of up to 2,500 or 3,000kg – despite this, the '88 continued to operate successfully from rough fields. Also worthy of note in this photo is the offset bomb-aimer's gondola with its flat bombing window beneath the aircraft's nose. (IWM HU92193)

A *Luftwaffe* Heinkel He115 B-1 being towed up a slipway. Export versions of the Luftwaffe's He115 floatplane were supplied to Norway and Sweden in 1939. Norway's fleet increased in 1940 when two German He115B-1s were captured during the German invasion and some were then used against the Germans. Some of the Norwegian machines fled to Scotland when Norway fell and served with the RAF on clandestine operations until 1943. By 1940, seventy-six aircraft had been built in several versions. The crew of three comprised a pilot, radio operator and navigator who was also responsible for aiming the bombs or torpedoes carried in the large internal bomb-bay. The type was finally retired from patrols in the Arctic in the summer of 1944. (IWM HU5006)

Mountain troops of the *Gebirgsjäger* about to emplane wave at a landing '*Tante Ju*' as the rugged Junkers Ju52 was nicknamed. The Ju52/3m was one of the greatest aircraft ever built. Though simple by modern standards with a fixed undercarriage and corrugated construction, the tough Junkers was built in great numbers and served in a variety of roles from bomber to ski-equipped airliner. The '3m' (for three engines or *motoren*) was developed from a single engine version of the same aircraft, the Ju52. The 3m version first flew in April 1932 and became the standard aircraft of *Lufthansa*. The military applications of this capable aircraft were clear to the German militarists who urged the development of a military bomber-transport version. The Ju52/3mg3e, powered by three BMW 525hp 132A-3 engines, could carry six 100kg/220lb bombs and had a faired gun position on top of the fuselage rear of the wing, and a primitive 'dustbin' turret, each mounting a 7.92mm/0.31in machine gun. As a transport it could carry eighteen troops or twelve stretchers. The Ju52 was used on all fronts on which the Third Reich fought and was a vital part of the Nazi war machine. (IWM HU92206)

A Heinkel He115B-1 twin-float seaplane pictured during trials in early 1940. Despite the fact that the type was, in many ways, obsolete at the start of the Second World War, the He115 continued in *Luftwaffe* service almost to the end of the conflict, with production restarting briefly in 1943. The He115 was developed as a torpedo-bomber, mine-laying and reconnaissance aircraft in the mid-thirties. The He115 VI (civil serial D-AEHF) prototype made its first flight in 1936 and in March 1938 this aircraft set eight speed records over 1,000 km and 2,000 km courses carrying various payloads up to 2,000 kg. The type was used by coastal reconnaissance units of the *Luftwaffe* and when war broke out dropped parachute mines in British waters. Defensive armament consisted of one fixed forward-firing and one rear-firing 7.9mm machine guns. (IWM HU5004)

A Heinkel He111 B-0 being serviced. This version was a pre-production model powered by 1,000hp Daimler Benz DB 600As. The first production He 111B-1s appeared in late 1936 and thirty were sent to fight in Spain with the Condor Legion. The Spanish connection continued for by the end of 1944, over 7,300 He111s had been built for the *Luftwaffe* while a further 236 were licence-built by the Spanish manufacturer CASA. The Spanish machines (designated CASA 2.111), were identical to the He111 H-6 produced in Germany and half were powered by Junkers engines supplied from Germany. The rest of the Spanish aircraft, built post-war, had Rolls-Royce Merlin engines. Spain continued to operate the Heinkel bombers until 1965. (IWM HU4999)

Ground crew prepare to load a second LT F5b practice torpedo beneath the fuselage of a Heinkel He111H-6. In early 1941 the *Luftwaffe* resolved to step up its anti-shipping attacks against British targets but found that bombs were not effective. Following extensive trials, the *Luftwaffe* found that the He111 was an excellent torpedo bomber and the He111H-6 was introduced in late 1941. In addition to six machine guns and two cannon, the aircraft could also carry two 765kg torpedoes. I./KG 26 was the first unit to equip with the new He111 variant. Following training at an Italian base, by June 1942 the Gruppe, based in Norway, were ready for action against Allied Arctic convoys. Convoy PQ 17 was virtually wiped out by the torpedo-dropping Heinkels. (IWM HU4994)

A pair of He111H-11s in flight. The H series was the major production model of the German bomber and was a re-engined development of the earlier P-series but powered by Junkers Jumo 211 series engines. There were many variants within the H-series but the H-11 shown was a modified H-10 night bomber. It had a fully enclosed dorsal gun position with a 13mm MG 131 machine gun for increased top protection and more defensive armament. The gondola beneath the fuselage contained two 7.9mm machine guns and the aircraft carried extra armour plating. The bomber could carry up 1,250kg of bombs externally. The H-series served in all major *Luftwaffe* offensives in the early part of the Second World War in Poland, Scandinavia, the Low Countries, France and the Battle of Britain. (IWM HU4993)

A Heinkel He111H-11 with bomb bay open, the underside of its wings blackened by the engine exhausts. The Heinkels' shortcomings were exposed when they came up against the more modern fighters of the Royal Air Force, the Spitfire and Hurricane. Although by sheer weight of numbers, the He111s did inflict much destruction on Britain during the early stages of the Second World War, losses mounted and the Heinkel was soon restricted to night operations and other specialised missions. Under cover of darkness during the Blitz of 1940-41, the He111 continued to perform as an effective bomber inflicting serious blows against its British enemies, including the devastating raids on Coventry. Due to a German decision to focus on mass production of existing weapons rather than investing in development of newer ones, the He111 laboured on long after it should have been retired. He111s were developed for use as torpedo bombers, glider tugs and troop transports and in the last year of the war served as air launch platforms for V1 flying bombs targeted against British cities. By the end of the Second World War, however, the He111 was used mainly as a transport aircraft. (IWM HU4992)

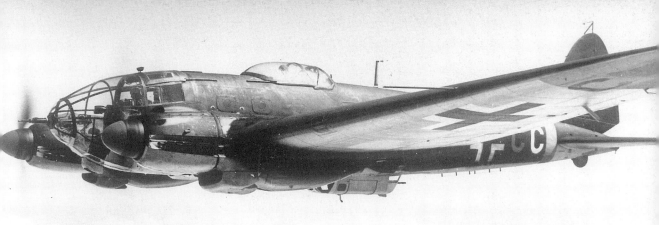

This fine air-to-air study shows a Heinkel He111H-16, one of a major production series. The H-16, a standard bomber version, was powered by two 1,350hp Jumo 211F-2 engines. It carried comprehensive defensive armament including twin MG 81Z machine guns, a 13mm MG 131 machine gun and an MG FF 20mm cannon. Sub-variants were the H-16/R1 with an electric dorsal turret, the H-16/R2 was a glider tug while the H-16/R3 was a pathfinder which could still carry a reduced bomb load. Features to note on the aircraft pictured are the large radiator bath air intakes beneath each engine, and the large glazed nose that offered excellent visibility but no protection. On bombing missions the bomb-aimer lay prone in the very front of the nose. The box-like protuberance beneath his position is the bombsight housing, offset to starboard. (IWM HU4991)

The Heinkel He177V-7 prototype – this machine was delivered to KG 40 at Bordeaux in August 1941 for operational evaluation. If the Nazis had successfully produced an atomic bomb, as the Luftwaffe's only heavy bomber, it would have been the He177 Greif (griffon) that would have carried it. At the end of the war a sole aircraft undergoing modification for the role was discovered in Czechoslovakia. Given the number of these aircraft that had to turn back from missions due to engine problems, the bomb may have posed more of a threat to Germany than anywhere else. Of all the aircraft in the *Luftwaffe*'s Second World War inventory, the He177 had the greatest military potential and caused the greatest amount of trouble to its crews. The aircraft was first proposed to meet a baffling 1938 requirement for a large, long range heavy bomber and anti-shipping aircraft that could deliver a sizeable 2,000kg bomb load in medium-angle dive bombing attacks. It has to be borne in mind that while the Allies embraced the concept of strategic air power as a means of waging war, the *Luftwaffe* was always a tactical air power provider to German land forces. That different philosophy explained the lack of large heavy bombers in the wartime *Luftwaffe* inventory. (IWM HU4990)

The Heinkel He60 was developed in 1932 as a reconnaissance aircraft to be catapult launched from large German warships. In reality, the type was used extensively by sea and coastal reconnaissance units well into the Second World War. Ruggedly constructed to cope with catapult launches and rough seas, the He60 first entered service in 1933. The unarmed He60A was the first version in *Kriegsmarine* (Navy) service, then the B model armed with a 7.9mm machine gun in the observer's cockpit appeared but was soon succeeded by the improved He60C that entered service in 1934. The C model was operated from most German warships prior to the Second World War - the aircraft's floats contained spraying equipment that could either lay down a smoke screen or spray mustard gas over enemy craft. The type was evaluated during the Spanish Civil War. The type was relegated to training duties early in the Second World War but it continued to serve in the maritime reconnaissance role with units in the Mediterranean, Crete and Greece. The aircraft pictured, was a Heinkel He60C but with armament removed became an He60D trainer.
(IWM HU2962)

Powered by two paired Junkers Jumo diesel engines, the rare Dornier Do26 was first designed to fly transatlantic mail services. When war came, the type was soon militarised for *Luftwaffe* service and, armed with cannon and machine guns, flew troops and supplies into fjords during the 1940 Norway campaign. Only five machines entered military service and of them two were shot down on May 28 1940 by British Hurricanes. The other three continued to fly during the Norway campaign but were withdrawn when lack of spares made their continued operation impossible. With a wing span of over 98 feet the Do26 was among the largest aircraft in the *Luftwaffe* inventory early in the war. (IWM HU2707)

The aircraft pictured is the Henschel Hs123 V2, registration D-ILUA, the second prototype of a neat and powerful dive bomber design begun in 1933. The 123 was a sesquiplane, a biplane in which the lower wing has less than half the area of the upper wing. The first production machines appeared in 1936 – armed with two machine guns the aircraft could also carry a 250kg bomb under the fuselage and four 50kg bombs under the lower wing. During December 1936, five Hs123s were shipped to the Condor Legion in Spain for evaluation in action in the Civil War. The type first saw action there in early 1937 but was soon eclipsed by the Ju87 Stuka. Nevertheless, the Hs123 continued to serve as a *schlachtflugzeug* or close support aircraft in Poland, France, Belgium and the Soviet Union as late as 1943. (IWM HU92207)

A DFS230A-1 glider pictured during trials with a Messerschmitt Bf109E fighter fixed to its top in place of a tow aircraft. Glider transport allowed troops to be set down in concentrated numbers, ready for combat virtually immediately. The DFS glider, if released by a tow aircraft at 10,000ft, could glide for a remarkable 35 miles. With a landing speed of only 40mph, the glider was usually stationary after a run of only 20 yards. The DFS230 was the only glider used by German forces up to and during the invasion of Crete. The glider could carry nine troops, a field radio and 3,000 rounds of ammunition or 7 soldiers, a machine gun, a handcart as well as ammunition and grenades. On 10 May 1940, forty-one DFS230 gliders were used in the first operational use of glider-borne troops for the German capture of the Belgian fort of Eben-Emael. For the invasion of Crete, fifty-three DFS 230 gliders were used. On 12 September 1943, twelve DFS230s were used to land troops to aid the escape of Mussolini from imprisonment in the Abbruzzi. (see page 72). (IWM HU92208)

Armourers at work on a Messerschmitt Bf109G-6. The G model, or 'Gustav' as it was known, was the most numerous of all the Bf109 versions. It became the standard version in *Luftwaffe* use after 1942 and used the more powerful DB605 engine mated to an F-series airframe. More than 30,000 Gustavs were produced in all, some licence-built in Hungary and Romania. The G was well-armed but was considered to need great attention from the pilot on landing. It served on all fronts in interceptor, ground-attack and fighter-bomber roles. (IWM HU92209)

This early production Heinkel He111B-2 is shown during a demonstration flight to showcase its manoeuvrability. The aircraft parked in the background is a Heinkel He112 fighter. The bomber is carrying the splinter type camouflage scheme worn by *Luftwaffe* bombers from 1936-40. This paint scheme featured dark brown, green and light grey on upper surfaces while the undersides were painted light blue. The He111 was developed while the *Luftwaffe* was still a secret from the outside world. The design brief had called for a fast airliner capable of adaptation to the bombing role as quickly and easily as possible. Heinkel's solution, proposed by twin designers Siegfried and Walter Günter was a scaled up version of their 1934 record-breaking single-engined He70 Blitz. The first prototype He111a powered by a pair of BMW VI OZ engines had its maiden flight on 24 February 1935. (IWM HU92210)

Known as the 'snow plough' to some but simply as a disappointment to others, this special version of the Heinkel He111 was developed to enable the *Luftwaffe* bombers literally to cut their way through the treacherous barrage balloon cables they encountered at lower altitudes over well defended British targets. The cutting rig extended from wingtip to wingtip and added considerable weight (250kg) to the Heinkel. These special conversions, thirty in all, of He111H-3 and H-5 aircraft were all designated He111H-8. The experiment was not considered a success after some operations over Britain with KG 54, although the modified aircraft were still able to carry a reduced bomb load. Some were subsequently turned into H-8R-2 glider tugs. (IWM HU92211)

This Heinkel He111H-5 was similar to the earlier H-4 but had greater range (due to fuel tanks replacing wing bomb cells) and could only carry its bomb load externally. This pictures shows the aircraft with a large 1000kg SC 1,000 bomb under its fuselage – it could carry two. This aircraft is operating on the Eastern Front in early 1943 and shows traces of a removable 'whitewash' layer of paint applied for winter operations over the standard camouflage scheme. The nose armament is probably a 13mm(0.51in) MG 131 heavy machine gun. It was this version of He111 that carried most of the heavy ordnance and parachute mines to Britain during the winter Blitz of 1940-41. (IWM HU92212)

The Heinkel He162 illustrates the desperate means to which the German military resorted in order to halt the Allied advance in 1944. One attempt was this small, cheap and easily built jet fighter designed to attack Allied bomber fleets as they pounded the Third Reich on a daily basis. The official requirement was issued in September 1944 and the whole programme, not just the aircraft, was given the name *Salamander*. Popularly known as the *Volksjäger* (people's fighter), the type first flew on 6 December 1944, incredibly, only thirty-eight days after detailed plans were first passed to the factory. The total time from the start of design work to the first test flight was just over six months. The aircraft pictured was an He162A-2 that was operated by JG1. After the aircraft was seized by US forces it was shipped to the USA for testing. (IWM HU4985)

The wartime caption for this photo said, *Spitfire pilots during their final training period were taken by the Intelligence Officer of the station to inspect a shot-down Junkers to enable them to obtain first hand information of a type of German aircraft which they will doubtless meet in combat.* On 15 August 1940 this Junkers Ju88 of 7/KG 30 left Aalborg in Denmark as part of a large force tasked with attacking RAF Driffield in Yorkshire. The aircraft, piloted by *Oberleutnant* Bachmann, was attacked by Spitfires of No. 616 Squadron when it reached the British coast and after both engines had been damaged, it force-landed near Hornby at 1.25pm. Three of the four crew were taken prisoner but the fourth had been killed in the engagement. During the attack, eight Ju88s were shot down but the bomber force still managed to drop 169 bombs on RAF Driffield and destroy eleven RAF bombers on the ground. (IWM CH1757)

A reluctance to lose aircraft production by introducing new types of aircraft characterised the German Air Ministry (RLM) decisions in 1943. Modification and improvement of existing designs was considered to be more cost and time effective than risky new projects. The Junkers Ju388 pictured was a derivative of the Ju188 which itself came from the Ju88. Junkers had already speculatively developed fighter, bomber and reconnaissance versions of the 188 which became the Ju 388. As high altitude reconnaissance was the greatest priority the Ju388L PR version was first to enter production with forty-seven delivered to the *Luftwaffe* by December 1944. The aircraft pictured is a Ju388K-1, one of only five production bomber versions made. The large wooden fairing below the fuselage covered the bomb load carried beneath the fuselage. A tail mounted rear warning radar was also fitted. (IWM CH15677)

A blazing Junkers Ju52 about to crash on Crete as German paratroops land on the island in May 1941. Crete was considered to be vitally important by the Germans who saw it as a means of dominating routes in the eastern Mediterranean. During the invasion, the *Luftwaffe* bombing of Heraklion Aerodrome was followed by ground strafing by fighters while others patrolled the bombed area to provide top cover for the troop-carrying aircraft that followed. Many of the German paratroopers were killed or wounded before they reached the ground. The paratroopers were men of the *Fallschirmjäger Regiment 1*. The surviving paratroopers' tenacity coupled with British errors enabled the German forces to take the airfields of Heraklion, Maleme and Canea. In the fighting for Crete the German paratroopers suffered over 5,000 casualties from a force of 13,000 and the *Luftwaffe* lost 220 aircraft including an incredible 119 Junkers Ju52s. The assault had been the first ever strategic use of airborne forces but one that Hitler was reluctant to use again due to the losses on Crete. (IWM A4155)

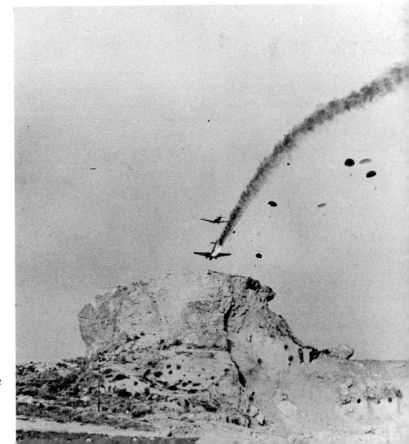

In the late summer of 1940, the Battle of Britain was at its height and London was adjusting itself to the shock of the *Luftwaffe*'s assault on the capital. This picture was taken on 7 September 1940, the day that *Luftwaffe* tactics in the Battle shifted. Having failed to destroy RAF Fighter Command by attacking its bases, the *Luftwaffe* began an all out onslaught against London. German thinking was that the British will to fight would break down as the population saw its capital being pounded day and night by the *Luftwaffe*. At around 4pm about 1,000 German bombers and fighters were detected on British radar screens, heading for London. This historic photo, taken on that day, shows two Dornier Do17z bombers over fires started by earlier attacking *Luftwaffe* bombers around London's Royal Victoria Docks and West Ham. (IWM C5423)

Luftwaffe Messerschmitt Bf109 fighters on patrol over the English Channel during the Battle of Britain. While the RAF had around 600 front line fighters, the *Luftwaffe* were able to field some 900 single-engined and 300 twin-engined fighters. A major disadvantage faced by the *Luftwaffe* fighter aircraft was that they were operating at the limit of their flying range from bases across the English Channel. Also, Britain's early warning radar, the most advanced system in the world at the time, gave the RAF warning of when and where to deploy their fighters, thereby avoiding standing aerial patrols in the wrong place. The aerial battles that took place over southern England during the historic summer of 1940 resulted in the Spitfires and Hurricanes of RAF Fighter Command becoming victors over their *Luftwaffe* adversaries. (IWM HU1215)

The problematic Messerschmitt Me210 appeared in response to a long-term requirement for a successor to the company's Bf110. The *Luftwaffe* wanted to retain a *Zerstörer* twin-engine fighter capability beyond the Bf110 and the Me210 design was awarded the contract. Following the first test flight, however, the aircraft was effectively condemned by test pilot reports as being vicious and hard to handle. The aircraft had to excel at air combat, ground attack, reconnaissance and dive bombing but almost seemed doomed at the outset. Problems were tackled while production was underway but were never resolved, so after 200 had been produced, the Me210 production programme was terminated. This was so serious, that the great Willy Messerschmitt himself was forced to resign. With a revised rear fuselage and wing planform as well as more powerful engines the design was salvaged and reappeared as the Me410 Hornisse (hornet) which entered *Luftwaffe* service in January 1943. The aircraft pictured is an Me210A-1. (IWM HU2741)

Messerschmitt Bf109G-2, serial 412951. Following the intense aerial battles of the Battle of Britain, the *Luftwaffe* called for single seat fighters with greater power. Developed in late 1941, the 'Gustav', or G model, was developed to use the 1,475hp Daimler Benz DB605 and could reach speeds of over 400mph at 28,500ft. The version had its combat debut in the summer of 1942 with fighter groups based near the English Channel. Compared to earlier models, the G had a stronger landing gear, a larger oil tank, and rear armour for the pilot together with increased head protection. The G could also be equipped with a drop tank or a bomb-rack. The G-2 model pictured dispensed with the pressure cabin introduced with the G-1 which was otherwise identical, both variants being armed with one 20mm MG151 cannon and two 7.9mm machine guns. This aircraft is fitted with an auxiliary fuel tank. (IWM CH15662)

Messerschmitt Bf109G of the famed *Jagdegeschwader* 53, or *Pik As*, literally the Ace of Spades. This was among the oldest fighter units of the Second World War with its origins going back to 1937. In May 1942 when the major campaign against Malta ceased, the '*Pik As*' *Geschwader* was split and its three *Gruppen* were deployed over three different theatres of operation. I JG 53 moved to the eastern front, where it took part in the offensive against Stalingrad. III JG53 saw service in North Africa in support of Rommel while II JG53, on Sicily, continued to try to stop British air and naval forces from interfering with the Axis shipping to and from North Africa. In late 1943, as German forces retreated north through Italy, JG 53 saw constant action over southern Italy and experienced heavy losses. The aircraft pictured is armed with two 20mm MG 151/20 guns under the wings in addition to normal armament. (IWM HU55218)

On Sunday, 21 July 1940 at 10:25am, this Messerschmitt Bf110 C-5. crash landed at Goodwood Home Farm following attacks by Hurricanes of No. 238 Squadron RAF based at Middle Wallop. The aircraft, based at Villacoublay in France, was an armed reconnaissance variant which had already shot down a training aircraft before it was itself attacked. Although the aircraft managed to evade its attackers, both of its Daimler Benz DB601 engines were damaged and eventually seized up. The crew, pilot *Oberleutnant* Karl Runde and *Feldwebel* Willi Baden, escaped from the aircraft unhurt following the landing and were captured. The aircraft, using parts from other Bf110s, was repaired by the RAF and was used for evaluation and training purposes. The photograph was taken on 6 September 1940. (IWM MH4194)

A Messerschmitt Bf109E in France late 1940. Despite the camouflage paint scheme, this aircraft's nose and tail appear to be yellow. The chevron markings on the aircraft's side tell us that this was the personal aircraft of the unknown unit's *Gruppen Kommandeur*. The 'E' model or Emil, as it was often known, was the definitive version of the Bf109. It was in action throughout the first year of the Blitzkrieg and, excluding the Spitfire, outclassed all the fighters it encountered. *Luftwaffe* 109Es first saw action against the Royal Air Force on 18 December 1939 during an attack on RAF Wellington bombers over Wilhelmshaven. Numerous versions of the Emil were in service during the Battle of Britain in 1940. (IWM HU44150)

Derelict *Luftwaffe* aircraft abandoned in the wake of Rommel's retreating Afrika Korps in 1942. The fuselages of Messerschmitt Bf109s and Junkers Ju88s, some of them bullet-ridden, line the road near Gambut. The second hulk with the RAF officer in the cockpit is a Bf109F-4/Trop in a *Luftwaffe* desert colour scheme of sand-yellow with olive green mottling. The aircraft's number 12 in yellow and the distinctive shield motif just forward of the cockpit and the horizontal bar to the rear of the *Balkenkreuz* national insignia, denote that this was an aircraft of 6.Staffel II/JG 3. Note the fuselage fifth away from the camera which appears to have been painted over with Royal Air Force insignia on the aircraft's side and tail. (IWM CM4038)

A wrecked Messerschmitt Bf109E-7/Trop, W Nr 6431, pictured near Sollum in Egypt late 1942. The aircraft crashed after being damaged in combat while covering the retreat of Rommel's troops. The aircraft had been on the strength of 8/ZG1, a *Zerstörergeschwader* twin-engined fighter unit, probably as an armed reconnaissance machine. The E-7/Trop was similar to the E-4/N, powered by a 1,200hp Daimler Benz 601N, but with provision for a 300 litre (66 gallon) drop tank or a 250kg bomb. The Trop version was 'tropicalised' by the installation of an Italian-designed dust filter over the supercharger air intake. The aircraft pictured was painted sand-yellow on its upper surfaces and sides while the undersides were painted sky blue. (IWM E19640)

Bf109E-1 (W Nr6296F) flown by *Oblerleutnant* Bartels, Technical Officer of Stab III/JG26 *Schlageter* pictured shortly after force landing in a wheatfield at Northdown, Kent on Wednesday, 24 July 1940. Bartels was severely wounded after an attack by a Spitfire of No. 54 Squadron from Rochford and did well to land the aircraft, although it came to land only yards from high tension power lines. In the engagement with the other aircraft of Stab III that day, a Spitfire was written off and its pilot killed while another Spitfire was damaged. The aircraft, though an E-1, had an E-4 canopy fitted retrospectively. The F in the aircraft's Werks number denotes that it has undergone a major overhaul. (IWM HU67707)

On 6 June 1938, the Heinkel He100 V2, registration D-IUOS and the second prototype of the design, with Ernst Udet at the controls, set a new 100km closed-circuit landplane world speed record. Heinkel were still smarting from the 1936 failure of their He112 in the competition against the Messerschmitt Bf109 in the *Luftwaffe* single seat fighter competition for which they proposed the He 100. The well publicised record-breaking flight did however cause some confusion in that the record-breaking He 100 was deliberately called the He112U in an attempt to generate interest in the genuine He112 being sold to Spain and Japan. On 30 March 1939, the He100V8 prototype set a new absolute world speed record of 463.92mph/746.6kph. Production fighter versions of the He100 did appear but the type did not enter *Luftwaffe* service. Service test pilots at Rechlin thought the aircraft, though wonderfully quick as a fighter aircraft, was hard to handle and had a high landing speed thus increasing the landing runs and the risks of accidents on the ground. Some He100s were sold to sympathetic nations (Japan and the USSR) together with permission for licence production. Twelve production machines were retained by Heinkel to defend one of their plants and were used for propaganda photos claiming to feature another high performance fighter in *Luftwaffe* service. In reality the He100 never fired its guns in anger. (IWM HU76169)

Excellently detailed photograph of the under-fuselage gondola of a Junkers Ju88R-1. The rear of the gondola is hinged down to allow crew access. The R-1 was a night fighter version of the Ju88 armed with seven machine guns. The chute on the top right of the photo was for dumping used cartridges from the nose armament out into the slipstream. Despite the presence of the swastikad Bf109 tail in the background, the author believes this is one of a number of detailed shots taken by the British at Farnborough of the R-1 whose crew defected in May 1943 with their aircraft. The aircraft, from *Nachtjagdgeschwader* 3 was flown from its base to RAF Dyce near Aberdeen, Scotland and was then flown on to Farnborough. (IWM HU23899)

Part Two

Air Crew and Ground Crew

Men of a *Luftwaffe* anti-aircraft unit at work on a range finder used to predict anti-aircraft fire. These optical devices worked in one of two ways to enable the users to calculate ranges, either coincidence or stereoscopic. Using coincidence the rangefinder split the target aircraft image into two separate pieces, usually one above the other; the two views were then moved into alignment to produce a range figure. The stereoscopic technique used two separate images of the target aircraft, one for each eye, that had to be merged together to get the correct range. These rangefinders were just a small part of the *Luftwaffe*'s extensive anti-aircraft system which, at its peak, employed 1.25 million personnel, such was the importance placed on it by the Third Reich. (IWM HU92638)

An *oberleutnant* aboard a Bv138 flying boat. These aircraft were powered by three Jumo diesel engines which, though economical, did not bestow great performance. Although the Bv138 could carry a small bombload or depth-charges, most operations were purely reconnaissance. The aircraft could defend itself though and the type was credited with the destruction of an RAF Catalina and a Blenheim. Some were later modified to carry out minesweeping duties. Most Bv138s were equipped with catapult points for operation from seaplane tenders and some were fitted with a modified fuel filter to remove seawater pollutants when refuelling from U-boats. (IWM HU92196)

The wartime caption reads, *The German anti-aircraft arm is equipped with the most modern listening equipment which can pick up the slightest sound of enemy aircraft.* At the beginning of the war, the most-used type of searchlight in the *Luftwaffe* was the 150cm *Flakscheinwerfer* 37. Operating in units of up to 64 lights, the ears of the searchlights were the sound locators, although the wider ranging fire-control radars that entered service later in the war were more effective. During 1942 the much brighter 200cm *Flakscheinwerfer* 40 entered service. These were usually positioned close to the radar. If searchlights were brought to bear on to a target aircraft and locked on then the aircraft was rendered useless as a bomber because the bomb-aimer was blinded. (IWM HU92197)

Over the target. A *Luftwaffe* film reporter switches on the camera, fixed in the fuselage of the bomber, when the target area is reached. What is not clear is whether the film was for propaganda or mission evaluation purposes. The Nazis were experts in the use of propaganda, a weapon of control, upon their own people. Hitler, who was aware of the value of good propaganda, appointed Joseph Goebbels as Minister of Propaganda and National Enlightenment. The *Luftwaffe* had been central to the effective use of blitzkrieg tactics and were largely responsible for early success in the campaigns in the west. The *Luftwaffe* in action was a popular topic for newsreels and Goebbels had to ensure that the German Air Force always appeared to be one to be reckoned with. This man wears the Type FL 30231 seat type parachute (*Sitzfallschirm*). The fact that it resembles the harness used by the RAF is no coincidence, as from 1937 the *Luftwaffe* contracted British company Irvin to supply parachutes. Following the outbreak of war Germany continued to copy and produce this system with very few modifications. (IWM HU92198)

On a night operation against England surely and accurately, the pilot flies his machine, heavily laden with bombs, in an attack against the industrial area of the Midlands . In 1940-41 the *Luftwaffe* carried out sustained bombing campaigns against London and other British cities in which over 43,000 British citizens lost their lives. The Blitz, though named after the German *Blitzkrieg* strategy of mobile offensive 'lightning' warfare, was most certainly not an example of this. While the Battle of Britain raged, the *Luftwaffe* had concentrated on the attempted destruction of the Royal Air Force although a limited bombing campaign against industrial and communications targets had been under way since mid-August 1940. On the night of 24 August 1940, German bombers intended for the oil refineries at Thames Haven dropped their bombs on central London. Churchill immediately ordered retaliatory attacks against Berlin which led to an escalation of the air war from both sides. (IWM HU92199)

This propaganda photo from mid-1940 had the caption, *Coastal defence along the Channel. The finely attuned ear of the A.A. listening apparatus picks up the hum of aircraft engines from the direction of the Channel.* The range of early German sound locators was around three and a half miles but as sound takes time to travel, aircraft tended to be a mile ahead of the location at which they generated their engine noise. Consequently the early 'listeners' were really only for last minute warning of fighter aircraft. As the war progressed Flak became more accurate and certainly more numerous. By 1942, around 15,000 88mm guns defended Germany as well as 37mm and 20mm guns. The 88s could fire a 10kg shell up to 10,600m at a rate of 15-20 rounds per minute. When the shells exploded at a preset altitude, they sent metal splinters flying in all directions at high speeds. (IWM HU92200)

An iron greeting for England. This photo shows Luftwaffe gorund crew bombing up a Heinkel He111. The Heinkel He111 bomber could carry some ordnance externally beneath its wings but the aircraft's two ESAC bomb bays, one either side of the walkway linking front and rear crew compartments carried bombs vertically. Standard load was eight 250kg bombs stowed nose uppermost as shown in the photo. The bombs being loaded here are in fact 50kg. In the early stages of the Second World War the majority of German High Explosive bombs dropped on Britain were 50 or 250 kg but gradually bombs of increasing size and weight were available to the *Luftwaffe.* (IWM HU54512)

German fliers in Sicily. Painting the squadron badge. A *Luftwaffe* airman paints the white cockerel emblem of *Zerstörergeschwader* 26 *'Horst Wessel'* onto a Messerschmitt Bf110. The arrival in Sicily of a large force of *Luftwaffe* combat aircraft was bad news for Malta. Already pounded, but not beaten, by the Italians, Malta now received such a sustained bombardment that the island itself was awarded the George Cross. By April 1942 the British had evacuated all aircraft and ships from the island, such was the ferocity and regularity of the attacks. This was a missed opportunity for Berlin. Had the Germans not still been smarting from the heavy losses of airborne troops in the invasion of Crete and invaded Malta it would surely have succeeded. (IWM HU92201)

The German caption for this read, *Preparations for the start despite cold and snow. The attack on England is carried out despite the difficulties caused by adverse weather conditions.* SC250 bombs can be seen beneath the Heinkel He111. The main types of bombs used by the *Luftwaffe* were types designated SC (*Spreng-Cylindrisch*, a thin-cased general purpose high-explosive weapon); SD (*Spreng-Dickewand*, thick-cased semi-armour piercing) and PC (*Panzer-Cylindrisch*, armour piercing). These type designations were a prefix, followed by a number indicating their weight in kilogrammes. e.g. SC250, SD500. Some of the larger German bombs had nicknames, for example, SC1,000 *Hermann* (named after Göring, chief of the *Luftwaffe*), SD1,000 '*Eseu*' (short for *Entseuchung* or mine-clearing). (IWM HU92202)

Officers and men of 2/KG77 at Freux auxiliary airfield in Belgium 1940. The aircraft in the background is a Dornier 17Z. As the *Luftwaffe* blitzed its way through western Europe the air force had to find bases as each step in the campaign was achieved. The military bases seized from the enemy were most sought after as they had permanent facilities, which, even after sabotage, were soon recommissioned. Auxiliary airfields like Freux may have had protective revetments built while *Luftwaffe* specialists would have ensured power requirements were met. Warning lights would have appeared on buildings nearby if not already in place. Accommodation for officers and men if not available on site 'would have been found in commandeered houses or hotels near the airfield. Piled to the side of the personnel are their personal clothing bags (*Bekleidungs-sacke*), indicating that they have just arrived or are about to depart. (IWM HU22370)

A march past at the *Luftwaffe* basic training school or *Fliegerersatzabteilung* at Neu Kuhren. After six months, recruits destined for flying training would move on to a *Fluganwärterkompanie* for around two months of general aeronautical tuition before moving on to elementary flying school. Wearing *Paradeanzug* (parade dress) these recruits pass out on completion of their basic training. Officers wear brocade belts, aiguillettes and swords while some recruits sport marksmanship shoulder cords. In the German tradition, Colours were carried by non-commissioned officers and escorted by junior officers. Note the *Fahnenträger* (colour bearer) carries the Colour and wears the brocade Colour belt. (IWM HU22478)

Early Second World War interior of the Officers' Mess at Oldenburg *Luftwaffe* base. Note the bust of Hitler. Pre-war messes of this type were frequently decorated with murals depicting the clandestine formation and development of the *Luftwaffe*. Oldenburg had a great military heritage and was the second largest garrison town in the Third Reich. Work on the *Luftwaffe* base began in the mid-1930s while the German Air Force was still secret. Initially a training station, the airfield later became a day and night fighter base. Later in the war the base was regularly attacked by Allied bombers and as the Allied troops prepared to overrun the airfield, leaflets were dropped on the defenders which said *We want to spare Oldenburg, because we will live here* . (IWM HU23725)

Leutnant Johannes Naumann, describing an air combat he had whilst his unit was engaged in protecting the *Scharnhorst* and *Gneisanau* together with other ships of the German Fleet during their February 1942 dash through the English Channel. Naumann was with III/JG26 at the time and flying the Focke-Wulf Fw190 seen in the photograph. (IWM HU38417)

Right: Excellent study of the crew at work within a Blohm und Voss Bv138 Flying Boat. The original German caption states that the *Oberleutnant* pictured at the centre was this aircraft's commander – note the rank patch on his left arm with the two pairs of wings and the white bar. Both men wear the LKp W100 winter flying helmet, a sheepskin-lined leather helmet that featured ear telephones and built in throat microphones. The *Oberleutnant* (left) wears Model 306 goggles (*Fliegerschutzbrille*). The Blohm und Voss Bv138 Seedrache (sea dragon) was unofficially referred to as *the flying clog* by its crews. The type served in the Atlantic, Arctic, Bay of Biscay, Mediterranean, Baltic and Black Sea and equipped a total of around twenty squadrons. All the crew are wearing standard fighter and bomber crew inflatable life jackets. Usually worn deflated, the jacket 'bladder' was inflated by opening a small compressed-air bottle attached to the lower left side of the jacket. The jacket could also be inflated orally by the black tube with a one-way valve seen fitted vertically on the front left side of the officer's jacket. (IWM HU92203)

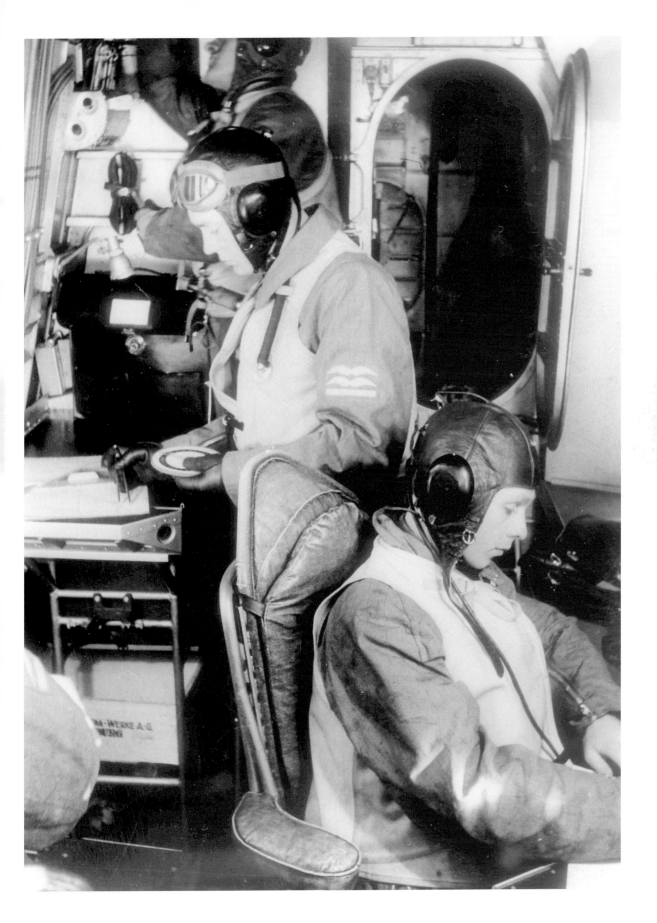

Part Three

Luftwaffe Operations

The caption of the time read, *Under the most dramatic circumstances, the Italian Head of State Mussolini was released from his imprisonment by the government of the traitor Bagoglio. Mussolini was liberated from the Grand Sasso in the Abruzzi mountains by men of the German parachute formations. The picture shows the Duce leaving his prison in a Fieseler Storch aircraft.* The special commando/special forces unit that carried out the audacious mission was commanded by Otto Skorzeny and was composed of *Luftwaffe Fallschirmjäger* (paratroops), *Sicherheitsdienst* (SS Security Service) and *Waffen SS.* (IWM HU92213)

When this photo was issued for propaganda purposes in 1941 the caption proudly proclaimed, *They bombed the Empress of Britain*. The largest ship ever built for the transatlantic route to Canada was the *Empress of Britain*. At more than 45,000 tons, the Canadian Pacific liner dwarfed her competitors. In peacetime, the *Empress of Britain* undertook winter cruises to exotic locations like Hong Kong and South America. On 26 October 1941 the crew (pictured) of a KG40 Focke Wulf 200 Condor, based in the South of France, found the *Empress of Britain*, impressed as a troop transport, at sea some 110km north west of Donegal. The *Luftwaffe* aircraft straddled the ship with bombs causing it to catch fire and a U-boat later sank her with two torpedoes. For leading the attack, the captain of the Condor, Bernhard Jope (pictured with flying suit) was awarded the Knight's Cross of the Iron Cross. (IWM HU54518)

Stuka pilots in the Mediterranean theatre being given their briefing. During the Battle of Britain the Stuka was found to be vulnerable to modern fighters but the type continued to serve. It was widely used during the fierce battle for Crete operating from Greek airfields. The invasion of Crete, Operation MERKUR, called for the Stukas to attack both ground targets in support of German paratroopers as well as Royal Navy ships. The officer, a *Leutnant* (centre) is wearing a private purchase leather coat, cut in identical style to the official cloth greatcoat and adorned with shoulder boards indicating his rank. These coats were permitted but at the officer's personal expense. (IWM HU92204)

The wartime caption for this photograph read, *A German Ju88 brings back the top of a ship's mast*. During a low-level attack upon a British destroyer, the top of the ship's mast tore the underneath part of the fuselage. The mast tip, however, remained in the aircraft's body. The machine made a successful landing. The picture shows the plate shaped torn-off mast tip of the British destroyer. An unusual war souvenir. The aircraft that had flown unfeasibly low over the ship was in fact a Heinkel He111. Piloted by a Major Harlinghausen during the Norwegian campaign, the aircraft attacked the SS *Sirius* in the Westfjord. Harlinghausen survived the war and served in the post-war *Luftwaffe* until 1961. (IWM HU92205)

The moment of impact as a road bridge at Volotov, 3kms east of Novgorod, receives a direct hit from a Stuka of I/Stuka 2 on 17 August 1941. On that day, German forces pushing towards Leningrad captured Narva. The Ju87D could carry an 1,800kg bomb beneath the fuselage and four 50kg or two 500kg bombs beneath its wings. Most Stukas were, however, armed with the 1,400kg armour piercing bomb or the 1,000kg general purpose weapon. (IWM HU24848)

This dramatic photograph shows a train burning after the attack by Ju87s of III /Stuka 2 on 8 July 1941 near Tuschkovo, on the line between Memel and Novosakoloniki. At this stage of the war in the East, *Panzergruppe* 4 had captured Pskov and advanced toward Novgorod and Leningrad. Elsewhere on that day, Germany and Italy announced the dissolution of Yugoslavia, with large portions of the country annexed by Italy. The independent state of Croatia, allied to the Axis and with its capital at Zagreb (Agram) was proclaimed on the same day. (IWM HU24841)

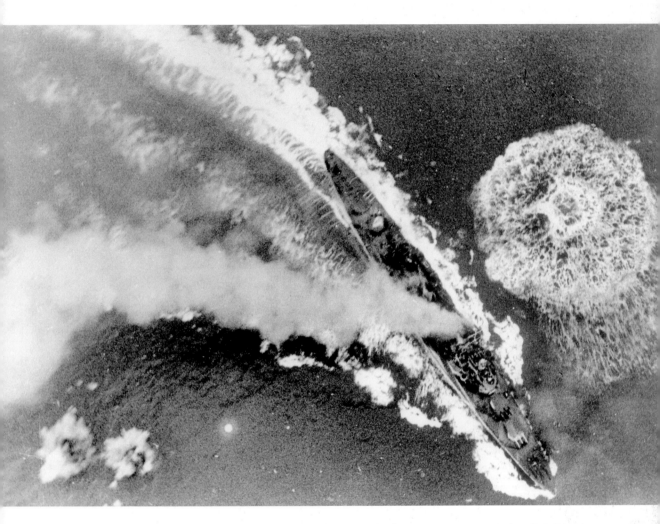

Photograph taken from an enemy aircraft during the attack on HMS *Gloucester* by *Luftwaffe* Ju87s and Ju88s on 22 May 1941. The ship can be seen taking avoiding action. The *Gloucester* was completed in January 1939 and in May 1940 joined the 7th Cruiser Squadron in the Mediterranean fleet based at Alexandria. In July 1940 *Gloucester* was damaged by an Italian air attack and her Commanding Officer, Captain F R Garside, was killed. Between August 1940 and May 1941 the ship was involved in many actions, and earned many battle honours as well as the nickname, 'The Fighting 'G''. In May 1941 while Royal Navy ships sought to prevent a German seaborne landing on Crete they were subjected to frequent attacks from the air. After repeated attacks and numerous direct hits, HMS *Gloucester* sank in the Antikythera Channel, north-west of Crete on 22 May 1941. In less than a year's service in the Mediterranean, HMS *Gloucester* had lost over 736 men, including two Commanding Officers. Admiral Sir Andrew Cunningham said, 'Thus went the gallant *Gloucester*. She had been hit by bombs more times than any other vessel, and had always come up smiling.' (IWM HU24829)

Part Four

Luftwaffe Images

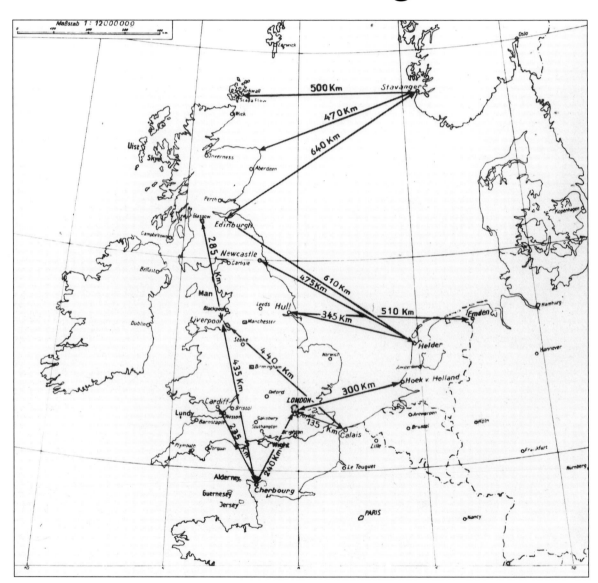

A pre-war *Luftwaffe* briefing map showing flying distances to a number of key points in Britain. Interestingly, the distances are calculated largely from points that Germany would have to invade before the *Luftwaffe* could make use of them. The German state airline *Lufthansa*, launched in January 1926, soon became one of the leading airlines in Europe. From the mid-1930s, however, the airline's activities over Britain were not always purely civil. Under the terms of the Treaty of Versailles 1918, Germany was not supposed to have an air force, so the *Luftwaffe* was covertly trained and organized using *Lufthansa* as cover. The air force's existence was officially announced on 1 April 1935. Photo mapping was undertaken by many of the German airliners and this proved invaluable later for targeting purposes. Equally, a number of German airline pilots familiar with the routes to and around Britain later joined the *Luftwaffe*. (IWM HU16202)

The 1938 caption for this picture describes it as, *The Mersey Bight near Port Ellesmere, near Liverpool.* The Manchester Ship Canal can be seen running from two thirds of the way up the frame on the right and running off the frame, top left, out into the River Mersey. The straight line running across the centre of the photo is a railway line. It is, however, the area between these two features that was of interest to the *Luftwaffe* – the Shell Petrochemical Refinery at Stanlow. Established in 1922, Stanlow was one of Britain's biggest oil refineries and its continued operation was vital for the British war effort. Reportedly, there was a German commercial mapping company operating around Liverpool pre-war and this may be one of their photos. By 12 December 1940, Merseyside had been subjected to 300 air raids. (IWM HU16205)

A pre-war vertical aerial photo of the centre of London. Among the points of interest noted on the photo are the Houses of Parliament (h), The Tower of London (e), The Oval cricket ground (o) and Hyde Park (c). Towards the end of the 1930s, *Lufthansa* operations in Britain had grown considerably. Operating from airports such as Croydon, *Lufthansa* aircraft would take off at night with spare crews on night training missions. Frequently, using bad weather as an excuse, *Lufthansa* pilots would fly near or even over RAF airfields including Biggin Hill and Kenley. The German airline staff continued to be based in Britain almost until war broke out. The last *Lufthansa* flight, a Ju52 departed Croydon on 31 August 1939. (IWM HU16281)

A reconnaissance photo of Birmingham, the city whose industry was so vital to the British war effort. Birmingham became, after London, the second most heavily bombed British city. 2,241 residents were killed while *Luftwaffe* action seriously injured another 3,010. *Luftwaffe* attacks began on 9 August 1940 and ended on 23 April 1943. 12,391 houses, 302 factories, 34 churches, halls and cinemas, and 205 other buildings were destroyed. Bomb damage reports were not, however, public knowledge as it may have served as feedback to the *Luftwaffe* who may have been able to refine or improve their bombing techniques. The role of the aircraft factory at Castle Bromwich, Birmingham, cannot be underestimated. By the end of the war, it was producing 320 Spitfires and 20 Lancasters a month – more than any other British factory. (IWM HU16288)

A pre-war photo of what the *Luftwaffe* described as, *...the Austin Aircraft works in the south of Birmingham.* The enormous Longbridge car plant had manufactured aircraft and other military equipment during the First World War so the Germans were aware of its potential during another war. In early 1940, Churchill's Chiefs of Staff told him that, *Germany could not gain complete air superiority unless she could not knock out our air force, and the aircraft industries, some vital portions of which are concentrated at Coventry and Birmingham.* During the Second World War the plant produced ammunition, tank components, steel helmets, Hawker Hurricanes, Fairey Battles, Horsa gliders, mines, depth charges and even Lancaster bombers – 2,866 aircraft in all. By 1944, around 400,000 of Birmingham's population were engaged in war work. (IWM HU16291)

This excellent oblique aerial photo shows the Manchester Ship Canal as it heads away from Manchester. In the foreground denoted by 'sa' can be seen Salford Quays. The *Luftwaffe* Blitz on Manchester over Christmas 1940 affected 50,000 homes in the city and left 596 dead and over 2,300 Mancunians injured, 719 of them seriously. More than 30 acres of land within a mile of Manchester Town Hall were destroyed in 1940. Manchester Cathedral was seriously damaged and the Manchester Royal Infirmary suffered a direct hit. Victoria Station and even Manchester United's football ground were not spared. 72,000 children were evacuated and did not return until much later in the war. (IWM HU16294)

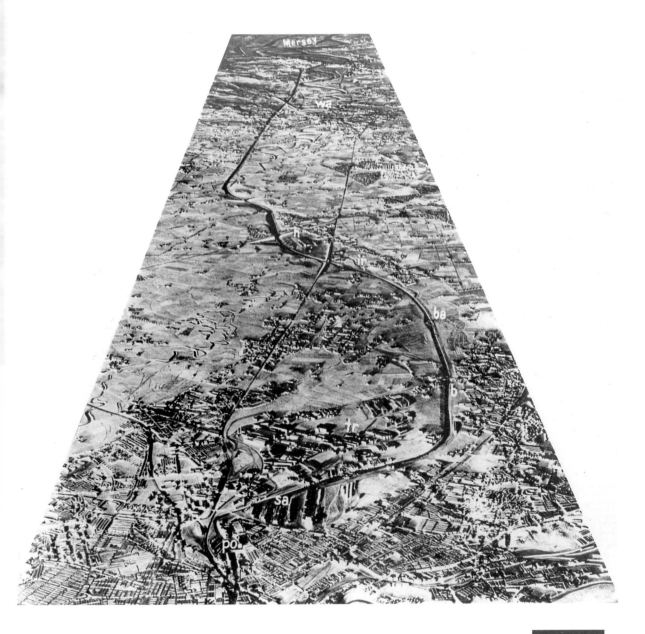

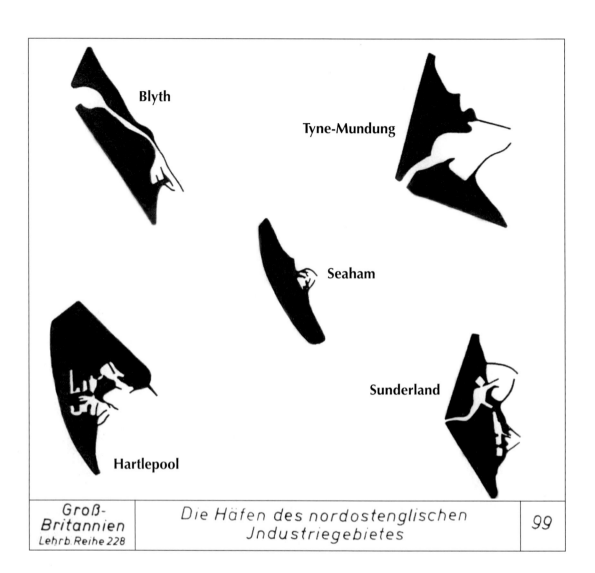

Blyth

Tyne-Mundung

Seaham

Sunderland

Hartlepool

Groß-Britannien Lehrb. Reihe 228	Die Häfen des nordostenglischen Jndustriegebietes	99

Pre-war silhouettes of harbours of north-east Britain used to train *Luftwaffe* navigators in preparation for attacks against industrial targets. It may appear obvious but it was important that *Luftwaffe* navigators could confidently identify potential targets. Some navigators were less able than others which accounted for bombs falling many miles from their intended targets or even German aircraft and their disorientated crews landing at British bases. The industrial centres of the north-east of England were prime targets for the *Luftwaffe*. Centred on the Rivers Tees, Tyne and Wear, they were relatively easy to identify from the air. The ICI works on Teesside was frequently attacked but never seriously damaged. Flying from bases in Scandinavia almost 400 miles away, the *Luftwaffe* began attacking targets between the Rivers Tyne and Humber in August 1940. In all, there were more than 250 *Luftwaffe* air raids on the North-East and North Yorkshire. (IWM HU16300)

Part Five

Luftwaffe Personalities

Johannes Muller (centre), Director of the AGO *Flugzeugwerke* in Oschersleben bei Magdaburg, meets Adolf Galland, late 1940. Muller was the father-in-law of *Oberleutnant* Erwin Axthelm, Battle of Britain pilot with JG51who was believed to have been shot down over England on 30 August 1940. AGO was used to manufacture both Focke-Wulf and Messerschmitt types under licence. This was necessary to disperse production as widely as possible but also simply to keep up with the demand from the *Luftwaffe*. Ultimate responsibility for aircraft production rested, until 1944, with the *Reichsminister der Luftfahrt* (State Minister for Air). The *Reichsluftfahrt Ministerium* (Air Ministry) which housed the *Luftwaffe* High Command was the umbrella organisation for both functions. Hermann Göring led both elements almost to the end of the Third Reich with the titles Commander in Chief of the Air Force and the State Minister for Air. (IWM HU38410)

Generalfeldmarschall Albert Kesselring (left) with Johannes Muller (centre), Director of the AGO aircraft plant. Oschersleben bei Magdaburg 1940. Despite the apparent efficiency of the Nazi war machine, there were serious shortcomings in terms of aircraft production but not just in numbers. Indeed, the numbers of aircraft produced throughout the war remained relatively high for Germany but the types in production were largely developments of the same types that had taken part in the Blitzkrieg against Poland. Germany really lacked the aircraft it needed to wage total war instead of the Blitzkrieg machines that it stuck to so doggedly. Had the *Luftwaffe* been equipped with long range, fast single-engine fighters and fleets of long range four-engined bombers that could have dropped heavy bombloads on British cities, industry and airfields in 1940 then the Battle of Britain may have taken a different turn. (IWM HU38413)

Reichsmarshall Hermann Göring addresses a group of *Luftwaffe* pilots during the Battle of Britain. During these visits he frequently chastised the senior officers if he thought they were underachieving or lacking in fighting spirit. It was during one of these visits to JG26 in September 1940 that Göring was involved in a discussion immortalised in the 1968 film *Battle of Britain*. When he asked Adolf Galland, CO of JG26 of his requirements for his unit, Galland simply replied, 'Spitfires'. Behind his back Göring is holding his unique ivory, gold and platinum baton. (IWM MH13382)

In this photograph taken on 12 September 1940, Göring's unique dove-grey cap and uniform contrast sharply with the conventional uniforms of his men. The *Feldwebel* (sergeant) he is addressing wears the *Luftwaffe* pilot qualification badge and the ribbon of the Iron Cross II Class in his tunic button hole. The NCO's rank is designated by the braid around his collar and shoulder straps combined with the single shoulder 'pip' and three 'wings' to his collar patches. (IWM GER1436)

Hitler pays a visit to the famous fighter group *Jagdegeschwader* 26 'Schlageter' at Abbeville on Christmas Eve 1940. Here the Führer is seen in conversation with the unit's Commanding Officer *(Geschwaderkommodore)*, Adolf Galland. Galland had combat experience in the Spanish Civil War, took part in the bombing of Guernica and flew a total of 280 missions. During the Battle of Britain, Adolf Galland became one of the *Luftwaffe*'s top aces becoming commander of JG 26 on 22 August, a position he held until December 1941. After the death of *Oberst* Mölders on 22 November 1941, Galland succeeded him as General of the German Fighter arm. The unit was named after Arnold Schlageter, an early Nazi 'martyr' executed by the French. (IWM HU74453)

Generalfeldmarschall von Richthofen (right) with *Oberst* Oskar Dinort (left), *Geschwaderkommodoren* of *Sturzkampfgeschwader* 2 'Immelmann', October 1941. Wolfram von Richthofen, a popular leader, had studied engineering after the First World War before rejoining the German Army. When Hermann Göring announced the formation of the *Luftwaffe* in 1933, Richthofen immediately joined and become one of the organisation's chief technical advisors. After the outbreak of the Second World War, Richthofen led the 8th Air Corps and in Poland directed the attempt to destroy Warsaw. He also played an important role in the development of Blitzkrieg tactics and the use of the Stuka. In April 1941, Richthofen provided air support for the German invasion of Greece and then commanded the 2nd Air Force in Italy before being sent to support Field Marshal Erich von Manstein and the Army Group South during the invasion of the Soviet Union. This photo was taken in that period. (IWM HU24784)

General von Richthofen salutes the *Reichsmarschall* (left) during Göring's visit to the Air Fleet commanded by the Red Baron's cousin. It was during this phase of his career that Richthofen was tasked with supplying General von Paulus and his 6th Army trapped at Stalingrad. Over a seventy-two day period the *Luftwaffe* delivered 8,350 tons of supplies. Casualties were high with 488 aircraft and over 1,000 crewmen lost. Meanwhile the 6th Army was decimated by enemy action or cold thanks to the ill-conceived strategies of Göring and Hitler which von Richthofen did his best to overcome. On 17 February 1943, Adolf Hitler made Richthofen Germany's youngest field marshal but by 12 July 1945 Richthofen was dead, not in combat but through a brain tumour. (IWM HU24785)

Generalfeldmarschall Wolfram Freiherr von Richthofen pictured during an inspection visit to *Sturzkampfgeschwader* 2 '*Immelmann*' in the autumn of 1941. As commander of *Fliergerkorps* VIII, von Richthofen built his reputation in close support air operations with the successful use of the Junkers Ju87 dive bomber. Von Richthofen's uniform tells of his First World War career – he wears the Great War honour title (*Kriegserinnerungsband*) at his right sleeve indicating previous service with his legendary cousin Manfred's distinguished fighter squadron during which he achieved eight victories. The title reads *Jagdgeschwader Frhr v. Richthofen. Nr.1 1917/18*. Subsequently he was the last commander of the *Legion Kondor* in Spain. (IWM HU24782)

Reichsmarschall Göring pictured during a visit to *Sturzkampfgeschwader* 2 'Immelmann'. The steel-helmeted soldier is Göring's personal standard-bearer and is seen carrying the *Reichsmarschall's* standard which is encased within its waterproof frame. The large Iron Cross symbolises that Göring was the only recipient of the Grand Cross of the Iron Cross during the Third Reich. The standard was introduced in July 1940. At the end of the war Göring was tried for war crimes, conspiracy, crimes against peace and against humanity. Found guilty, he was sentenced to be hanged but committed suicide on 15 October 1946. (IWM HU24783)

Generalfeldmarschall Albert Kesselring boarding the personal Siebel Fh104 Hallore he used to travel around France in 1940. Despite the failure of the *Luftwaffe* to achieve air superiority over Southern Britain in 1940, Kesselring's career did not suffer, which said much about this shrewd soldier's political skills. In 1941 he assumed command of German air forces in North Africa, where, with Rommel, he took the Allies to the brink of defeat. In Italy, from 1943, Kesselring showed himself to be a brilliant military commander. With overall command of air and ground forces, he managed to delay the Allied advance by a year. Convicted of war crimes, Kesselring was imprisoned for five years after the war and was released in 1952. (IWM HU38405)

Kesselring (left) with other officers inspecting an airfield occupied by JG 27 in early 1940. Bavarian born Kesselring served with the artillery in the First World War and became involved with aviation late in his career, transferring to the *Luftwaffe* in 1933. At the beginning of the Second World War Kesselring commanded the *Luftflotte* (air fleet) responsible for supporting the Army invading Poland. After this invasion and those of Norway and the Low Countries, he was given command of the northern of the two air fleets facing Britain. *Luftflotte* II was much larger than the southern *Luftflotte* III, and was the nearest command to Britain, such was the faith in Kesselring. The white stripes on Kesselring's uniform trousers indicate the rank of General – note also the *Luftwaffe* officer's dagger he wears. (IWM HU38406)

Hermann Göring was born in Bavaria on 12 January 1893. The son of a senior army officer, he attended a military school and became a member of the Prussian Cadet Corps. Göring joined the German Army in June 1912 and served with the infantry during the first months of the First World War. After being hospitalised with rheumatoid arthritis in his knees, he transferred to the German Army Air Service. Göring initially served as an observer but later became a pilot flying reconnaissance and then fighter types. He scored his first victory on 16 November 1915 and in July 1918, Göring became commander of his *Jagdegeschwader Richthofen*. He ended the First World War with twenty-two victories. After the war, Göring worked for a time as a pilot for the Fokker company based in Holland. (IWM HU23749)

Adolf Galland and Rolf Pingel pictured at Wissant, France during the Battle of Britain in 1940. Galland is sporting his trademark cigar for which he had cigar lighters installed in his personal aircraft. The *Luftwaffe* were buoyant until the Battle of Britain when they first met widespread opposition from the RAF. German invasion barges assembled in Channel ports, so confident was the German High Command of victory. However, long range fighter cover for *Luftwaffe* bombers was only partially available from German fighter aircraft operating at their limits from cross-channel bases. On 15 September 1940, RAF defences destroyed 185 German aircraft giving the *Luftwaffe* the clear message that air supremacy was not achievable over Britain. Both Galland and Pingel are wearing the standard Luftwaffe suede and leather fleece-lined flying boots. (IWM HU37973)

Luftwaffe fighter ace Adolf Galland, then CO of JG26, pictured in mid-October 1940. The tail of his Bf109 fighter carries forty-five victory symbols, the last being a No 46 Squadron Spitfire near Rochester. Galland is showing his aircraft to Italian Air Force officers which makes this photo part of an often overlooked aspect of post- Battle of Britain history. In late 1940, Italian CR.42 Falco biplane fighters were based in Belgium to escort Italian bomber attacks on Britain. The episode climaxed on 11 November when the only major Italian raid saw the attackers get a severe mauling from defending British fighters. Falcos were no match for Hurricanes or Spitfires. (IWM HU37976)

Werner Mölders (in the foreground facing camera) returns from combat – he was the leading *Luftwaffe* fighter ace during the Battle of Britain. Having gained combat experience in Spain, Mölders became a master tactician, pioneering the *rotte* and *schwarm* formations in which fighters flew in pairs and fours respectively. His tactics were so well demonstrated that the *Luftwaffe* fighter force adopted then across the board while other air forces including the RAF were using ponderous wing formations. By the Fall of France Mölders had shot down a total of twenty-five aircraft. During the Battle of Britain, Mölders commanded *Jagdeschwader* 51, and by mid-October 1940, had shot down forty-five RAF fighters. It was far from plain sailing, however, and RAF ace Sailor Malan raked Mölders aircraft with gunfire during a dogfight, injuring the German ace who survived the crash landing. His victory tally had reached 115 when, on 22 November 1941, he was killed in a crash caused by bad weather. (IWM HU37977)

Hauptmann Rolf Pingel, Adolf Hitler, and *Oberst* Adolf Galland, pictured at the Abbeville base of JG26, 24 December 1940. Pingel was a *Gruppenkommanduer* of I/ JG 26 until he was shot down in his Focke-Wulf Fw190 and taken prisoner on 10 July 1941. At the time of his capture he had flown 550 combat missions, including 200 in Spain, and was credited with the destruction of 28 aircraft. Hitler and Galland were to meet many times over the coming years but under the Führer's influence, in early 1945, Galland was appointed commander of a new fighter unit flying the Me262 jet, *Jagdverband* 44. Galland flew his last wartime mission on 26 April 1945 when he shot down his last victim, a Martin B-26 Marauder, bringing his total of victories to 104. (IWM HU37979)

Reichsmarschall Hermann Wilhelm Göring pictured here with *Luftwaffe* fighter ace Werner Mölders (right). Göring was a larger than life character who had had a distinguished First World War fighter-pilot career. At his throat Göring wears the unique Grand Cross of the Iron Cross, the Knights Cross and the *Pour le Mérite*. His unique dove-grey uniform was ordered by him after his elevation to the rank of *Reichmarschall der Grossdeutchen Reichs* by Hitler following the early victories in the West. The photo was taken after March 1941 when Göring had new collar patches made for the uniform. As the war progressed, Göring's power waned and in April 1945 he was sacked from his many posts following an attempt to take power from Hitler. (IWM HU4481)

Part Six

Luftwaffe Personnel

Before Germany could attack the Low Countries and then France, they first had to invade Denmark and Norway to prevent British and French troops occupying the countries. The Blitzkrieg attacks on Scandinavia were expected to be swift and decisive with the Danish and Norwegian air forces posing little threat. The campaign in Norway however lasted longer than expected and before Norway fell, 260 *Luftwaffe* aircraft were lost including 86 transport aircraft. The Stuka was a key element of the Blitzkrieg. The wartime caption for this propaganda photo stated, *Heroes of the Norwegian campaign receive the Knights Cross. Four Knight's Cross holders from a Stuka squadron, from left to right, Hauptmann Hozze, Leutnant Mobus, Leutnant Schafer and Feldwebel Grenzel.* (IWM HU92194)

Oberst Oskar Dinort, *Geschwaderkommodore of Sturzkampfgeschwader* 2 'Immelmann', from 15 October 1939 to 15 October 1941. Dinort, a record-breaking glider pilot became the first commander of StG 2. He received his Knight's Cross (*Ritterkreuz*) on 20 June 1940 during the campaign in the West. Dinort became the twenty-first recipient but the first Stuka pilot to receive the Oak Leaves to the Knight's Cross on 14 July 1941. At the war's end he held the rank of *Generalmajor*. It was Dinort who suggested the modification to Stuka-carried bombs known as *Dinortstabe* (Dinort's rods). 60cm metal rods were welded to the front of the bombs, with an 8cm metal disc on the end of the rod. On hitting the ground the rods caused the bomb to explode 30cm above ground causing much higher casualties among the enemy. (IWM HU24777)

Born in July 1912, Hubertus Hitschold first flew in 1930. After the conclusion of his basic training, Hitschold was posted to the secret training base at Lipetsk in the USSR. He transferred to the *Luftwaffe* in 1935 and in 1937 began his long association with the Ju87 Stuka. When war broke out in September 1939 Hitschold was in action almost immediately with the Stukas in Poland. On 1 October 1939 he was made *Gruppenkommandeur* of I/StG1. For his actions during the Blitzkrieg against Belgium, Holland and France, Hitschold, already an Iron Cross holder, was awarded the Knight's Cross on 21 July 1940. He is pictured here as a Major when he was a *Gruppenkommandeur*. By the end of the Second World War, Hitschold was a general. (IWM HU24778)

Hauptmann Ernst-Siegfried Steen, *Gruppenkommandeur* of III/ Stuka2. Steen was killed during the German actions near Stalingrad on 23 September 1941. At this stage in the campaign his unit was based at Tyrkowo and was equipped with the Ju87R. On 17 October he was posthumously awarded the *Ritterkreuz* or Knights Cross. Steen is seen wearing the *Fliegerbluse*, a plain, hip-length blue-grey jacket with fly-front and no visible buttons. Note the unusual variation of the Iron Cross 1st Class made of cloth and said to be more practical in the confines of a cramped cockpit. Steen also wears the Air-to-Ground Support operational flying clasp. (IWM HU24779)

Oberleutnant Karl Heinz Lutze (left) and *Oberleutnant* Werner Lode of *Kampfgeschwader* 77 at Freux auxiliary airfield in Belgium during the Blitzkrieg, 1940. On 27 September 1940 Lutze's Ju88A-5 was sent to attack London. At 15:30 the aircraft was brought down by a combination of ground defences and RAF fighters and crashed at Vexour farm, Penshurst near Tonbridge. The aircraft, coded 3Z+DC, was first hit by anti-aircraft fire over London, damaging the starboard engine. Hurricanes of Nos 229 and 249 Squadrons then attacked the aircraft , finally bringing it down. *Oberleutnant* Lutze, *Feldwebel* Adler and *Feldwebel* Zeller were killed in the crash but *Unteroffizier* Brodbeck baled out and survived to be taken prisoner. Both men wear the one-piece summer lightweight flying suit. While fighter pilots wore two-piece protective clothing over their uniforms, bomber and reconnaissance crew conventionally used one-piece suits. Both men are wearing the highly practical officer-pattern flying cap (*Fliegermutze*), distinguished by its high quality cloth, the silver aluminium piping around the edge of the curtain, and the wire embroidered badges. (IWM HU22366)

Officers of 2/KG77 at Freux auxiliary airfield, Belgium. Imported Fiat CR.42 biplane fighters were delivered to Belgium, disassembled, in March 1940 still carrying Italian camouflage. When, on 10 May 1940, Nazi Germany launched its assault on the Low Countries, Belgium's Aéronautique Militaire had received 25 CR.42s. Some of the Belgian defenders were woken at 01:15 in readiness for what was a not totally surprise attack and the gallant Belgian defenders were ordered closer to the German border. At 04:15, as the last fighters were leaving their runway to get nearer the enemy, the *Luftwaffe* Stukas appeared. With little experience of their new machines, the Belgian pilots did their best to stem the flow of the invaders who thought they were being attacked by Gladiator biplanes and not the Fiat fighters. Before Belgium fell, its air force destroyed or damaged a number of fighters, bombers and transports. (IWM HU22372)

Junkers Ju88 3Z+DM of *Kampfgeschwader* 77 photographed at Reims, France, in the winter of 1940-41. Within a couple of months this aircraft was shot down near Littlehampton on the south coast of England on 13 March 1941. The crew at the time of the photo are named from left as: *Oberleutnant* Werner Lode (pilot), Billesfeld (navigator observer), Waraczyneke (radio operator) and Wallner (gunner). The Junkers Ju88, though versatile and the fastest of the principal *Luftwaffe* bombers was found to have poor defensive armament. Long-winged Ju88A-4s were built with elongated wings to carry heavy bomb loads of up to 3,000kg. The four *Luftwaffe* aircrew wear the velveteen-collared electrically heated one-piece flying suit (*Winterfliegerkombi*). (IWM HU23722)

Above and right, *Leutnant* Karl Heinz Thurz at the controls of a Heinkel He111H-2, 1940. Thurz's active duty ceased on 17 January 1941 when his aircraft , damaged by RAF Hurricanes, crashed on Fair Isle. Thurz had lifted his Heinkel from the runway at Oldenburg in Germany at 08:00 to carry out a weather reconnaissance mission to the Faroes. Three hours into the flight the German bomber was attacked by two RAF Hurricanes and suffered serious damage. Having decided to head for safety in Norway, Thurz had to revise his plans when an engine failed and the undercarriage dropped. The Heinkel's second engine then failed and the pilot aimed for Fair Isle where he managed to crash land. Two of the five crew died in the crash and the survivors were taken to Lerwick Jail. Before being shipped to London for interrogation Thurz was introduced to the two RAF pilots who had shot him down. He was eventually shipped to Canada where he spent the rest of the war in a Prisoner of War camp. Much of Thurz's aircraft still survives on Fair Isle. (IWM HU23746)

Leutnant Karl-Gottfried Nordmann, of JG 51 who, by the end of war, was credited with 78 victories. As *Staffelkapitan* of 3/JG77, Nordmann took part in the campaigns in the Netherlands, Belgium and France and, finally, from July 1940, in the Battle of Britain. In 1941 Nordmann was in action over the Eastern Front achieving numerous victories bringing his total to 31 and on 20 July 1941 he became Kommanduer of IV/JG 51. More aerial victories followed swiftly and on 16 September 1941 after downing his 59th foe he was awarded Oak Leaves to his Knights Cross. On 10 April 1942 Nordmann was made *Geschwader Kommodore* of JG51. In January 1943, by then credited with 78 enemy aircraft, Nordmann was involved in an aerial collision with another JG51 pilot and his injuries forced him to leave front line duties. Nordmann survived the war and emigrated to the US where he died in 1982. (IWM HU37975)

Messerschmitt Bf109E pilots gather during the conquest of Scandinavia, 1940. From left to right; *Feldwebel* Ernst Arnold, pilot with back to camera – unknown, *Leutnant* Erwin Axthelm, *Feldwebel* Heinz Beushausen. The latter was killed over the English Channel on July 20 1940 flying with 3/JG27, shot down by pilots of No 238 Squadron RAF. The German invasion of Norway and Denmark was planned to be so swift and so hard-hitting that only thirty Messerschmitt 109s of JG77 were deployed in case of unexpected enemy fighter activity that could not be dealt with by the twin engine Bf110s. The single seat fighters made their way to the front line from the airfields of Husum to Aalborg and Esbjerg in Denmark before crossing to Kristiansand-Kjevik in southern Norway. (IWM HU38414)

Johannes Naumann was a young pilot with III/JG26 at the beginning of the war and flew during all the Blitzkrieg campaigns of 1939 and 1940, including the Battle of Britain. In March 1944 he was promoted to Kommandeur of II/JG26 and joined JG7 in April 1945. Johannes Naumann flew 450 combat missions, achieved forty-five victories, all in the west, and was awarded the Knight's Cross in 1944. (IWM HU38418)